MW00380801

Tried and True ESL Lessons
Level 2 Book A

Time Saving Lesson Plans for Instructors

Barbara Kinney Black

Copyright © 2017 Barbara Kinney Black
All rights reserved
ISBN: 1975754476
ISBN-13: 978-1975754471

DEDICATION

A dedication can only be to my Lord Jesus Christ who is the 'author and finisher of our faith' and the One who directed the writing of this volume.

CONTENTS

ACKNOWLEDGMENTS

Special thanks to my husband for his unending patient assistance, his photographic skill, and attention to detail in the editing process. Also, for assuming numerous tasks during the writing process.

To The Instructor

Welcome to Tried and True ESL Lessons, Level 2, Book A: Time Saving Lesson Plans for Instructors. I'm so glad you've decided to give us a try. Tried and True is exactly as its name states: **fully developed ESL lesson plans** compiled from 25 years of classroom teaching experience.

What Tried and True ESL Lessons Time Saving Lesson Plans for Instructors Can Do for You

- Guides the instructor in classroom presentation.
- Eliminates the need for instructors to write a weekly lesson plan.
- **Frees up the instructor** to concentrate on ministry to the students both inside and outside of the classroom.
- Serves as **a model for instructors** and ministries who wish to develop their own customized curriculum designed for their specific ministry environment.

Why Tried and True ESL Lessons Time Saving Lesson Plans for Instructors Came to Be

First, here's a little background of how Tried and True came to be. In my church, we prayed for 11 years to be able to begin an ESL ministry to internationals. After waiting for a church building in which to hold classes, we finally received the green light. The ministry began with four volunteers. We taught for six months and averaged 35 students weekly. At the end of the year, two of the volunteers were unable to continue, so the ministry was shelved.

Eighteen months later, the pastor approached me about beginning the ministry again. We knew the **biggest obstacle** was going to be finding volunteers who possessed enough time and expertise to plan quality lesson plans week to week. The pastor expressed surprise that the vast majority of ESL ministries currently depend on teachers to write their own lesson plans weekly. The pastor wondered why ESL teachers should have to write lesson plans while Sunday School teachers usually do not. Then the pastor asked me to write all the lessons for the teachers. Well, I was **a bit put off** and started to protest, but **the Holy Spirit nudged me** and said, "Be quiet and listen." The pastor made his case, and by the end of our meeting, I heard myself agreeing to write four levels of lesson plans weekly.

As soon as we announced the ministry training workshop, 40 volunteers signed up to attend training. At the completion of the training, 35 trained volunteers signed on to the ministry. **Most had little or no teaching experience**, but were willing to teach since a lesson plan would be provided to them.

What a **fantastic experience**! We soon had six levels of classes with 145 students attending weekly. Yes, it was a lot of work for me, but what rewards to **see volunteers learning to teach** and reach out in ministry to internationals. Incidentally, as a result, two volunteers became ESL teachers in addition to their church ministry.

Barbara Kinney Black

What's in Level 2, Book A

Most church based ESL ministries meet one time per week for a 1 ½ - 2 hour session. These sessions generally follow the public school calendar from Labor Day to Memorial Day with a Christmas break. This totals about 30 weeks of instruction. The Fall semester has about 13 weeks and the Spring semester about 16 weeks. **Book A with its 13 lessons** is a perfect fit for the Fall semester, but can be used at any time of year.

Lessons utilize a **functional approach** to language learning with an emphasis on simulating real life language situations. Students learn real language through a lot of **speaking and communication practice activities**. All lessons contain relevant material practical for everyday life in an English speaking country. They also contain a **biblical principle** related to the content of the lesson.

The **student book** is titled, Tried and True ESL Lessons Time Saving Lesson Plans for Instructors, Level 2 Book A. **Lessons are 8-10 pages** in length and feature vocabulary supported by pictures for comprehension, speaking, listening, grammar, pronunciation, and communication practice activities. There are also assignments in each lesson to do outside the classroom designed to reinforce language learning.

The instructor edition features an **Activity Bank** to guide instructors in **how to conduct** the Let's Practice communication activities. Any additional materials needed are very minimal and easily accessible. An alternate is usually suggested, as well. **Techniques** for presenting pronunciation and drilling vocabulary are included.

Since many ministries and students tend to operate on a limited budget, every consideration was made to keep the cost of Tried and True at the absolute bare minimum. Therefore, both instructor and student editions are published in black and white in order to make the program **very affordable**. For this reason, please note this is NOT a reproducible text.

Tried and True offers an additional resource book of **full color photos** of the vocabulary for comprehension which appear in both the student and instructor editions in **black and white**. This **optional resource book of color photos,** Tried and True ESL Lessons Time Saving Lesson Plans for Instructors Resource Manual is designed to support comprehension and further enhance the instructor's presentation and students' clear comprehension.

So, once again, welcome to Tried and True. **I pray** your experience with this curriculum will be a rewarding one whether you are a **brand new instructor**, **or a seasoned veteran**. To God be the glory!

Because of Him and them,

Barbara K. Black
M.S. T.E.S.O.L.
Contact us:
Email: bekblack19@gmail.com
Web: TriedandTrueESLResources.com
Facebook: Tried and True ESL Resources

Tried and True ESL Lessons
Level 2 Book A

Time Saving Lesson Plans for Instructors

By Barbara K. Black

Scope and Sequence

Unit-Lesson	Topic	Skills	Grammar
Personal Communication			
1-1	Introducing Self	Introducing self & country from	To Be Verb
1-2	Physical Characteristics	Describing physical characteristics with adjectives	Descriptive Adjectives
The Community			
2-1	911 Emergency	Reporting emergencies to 911	Present Progressive Tense
2-2	Where's the Mall	Asking for & describing location of places in the the community	Prepositions of Location
Let's Eat			
3-1	At the Deli	Ordering at a deli	Using WOULD LIKE
3-2	The Six Food Groups	Identifying foods in the six food groups	Using SOME and ANY

Unit-Lesson	Topic	Skills	Grammar
		Shopping	
4-1	I Went Shopping Today	Describing clothing by article, size, color	Past Tense Verb BE Word Order of Descriptive Adjectives
4-2	Black Friday Shopping	Identifying types of stores and products	Using BE GOING TO for Future Plans
		Housing	
5-1	Moving In	Describing placement of furnishing in rooms	Imperative Commands Demonstratives
5-2	Home Renovations	Describing common home renovations	Using WILL for Future
5-3	Home Repairs	Describing home repair attempts & calling a repair person	Questions with DO and BE
		Medical	
6-1	Healthy Living	Understanding doctor's advice for healthy behavioral changes	Using SHOULD to give advice
6-2	Staying Well	Describing medical symptoms and preventative measures	Using AND to Connect two ideas that are similar

Tried and True ESL Lessons

Level 2 Book A

Time Saving Lesson Plans for Instructors

UNIT 1 – PERSONAL COMMUNICATION – LESSON 1 – INTRODUCING SELF
STUDENT BOOK PAGE 1

A. Prayer for Students & Self

B. Lesson Objective and Functions:
   - Introducing self and country from

C. Grammar Structures:
   - TO BE Verb

D. Biblical Reference or Principles:
   - Exodus 3:13-14

E. Materials & Preparation:
   - A world map would add visual interest. Alternately, use the Internet to locate maps of the countries listed in the vocabulary

<u>Introduction</u>

Instructor introduce yourself including name and where you are from.
Ask a student his/her name and where they are from.
Repeat same with two more students.
Have students introduce themselves to a partner.
Say: "Today we are going to introduce ourselves."

UNIT 1

PERSONAL COMMUNICATION

LESSON 1 – INTRODUCING SELF

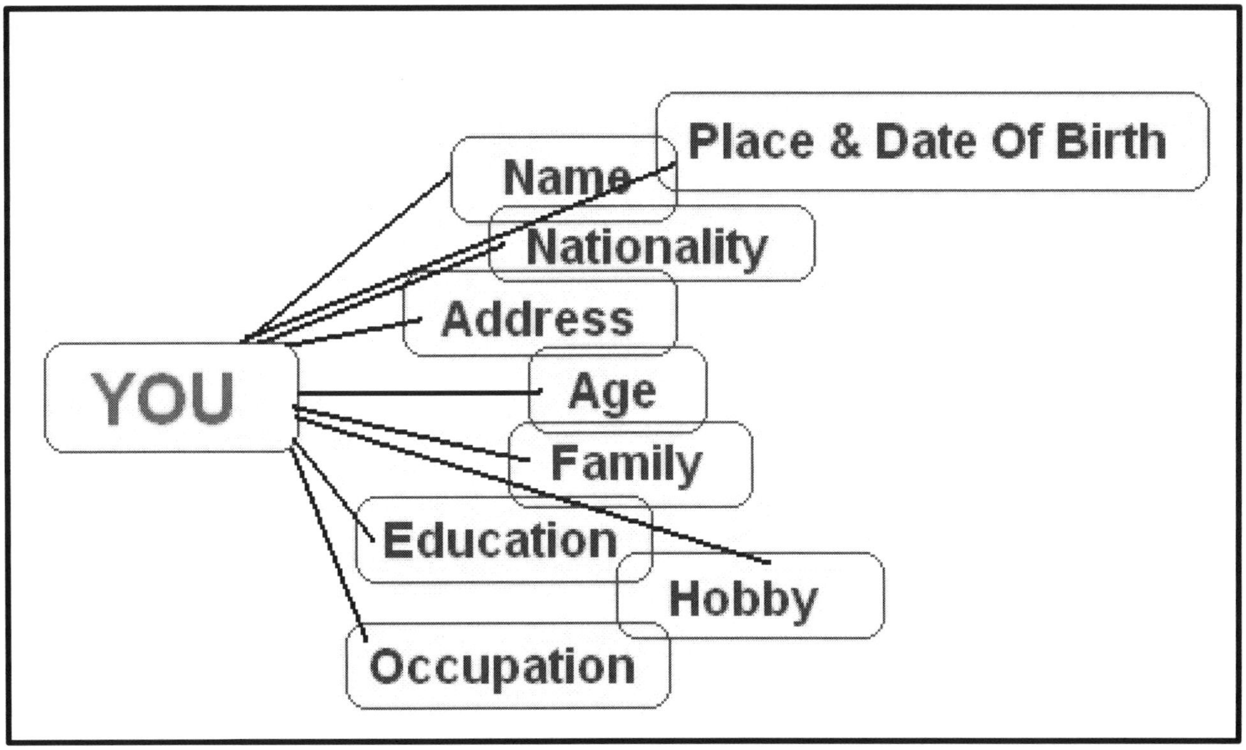

Hello, my name is Barbara.

UNIT 1 – PERSONAL COMMUNICATION – LESSON 1 – INTRODUCING SELF
STUDENT BOOK PAGE 2

Introduce New Vocabulary

1. Have students open to Unit 1 – Personal Communication; Lesson 1 – Introducing Self.
2. Introduce the words or phrases with a repetition drill. For instruction on conducting repetition drills, see Activity Bank. Repeat each 5-6 times.
3. Elicit conversation from students by asking questions such as, “Has anyone been to India or Korea,” and other countries introduced in the text.
4. A world map may be helpful to locate the countries in the text. Google images may be an option.
5. Discuss the importance of a firm handshake and what it says nonverbally. Also discuss the importance of looking into the eyes briefly of the person to whom you are speaking. NOTE: Demonstration of the handshake will take place later during Time to Practice activities.

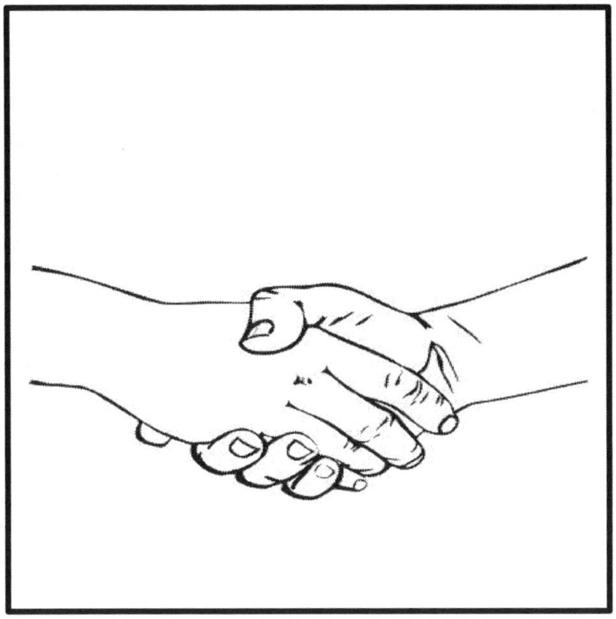

shake hands

Hello

My name is

Shawn

introduce yourself

Shawn – I'm from India

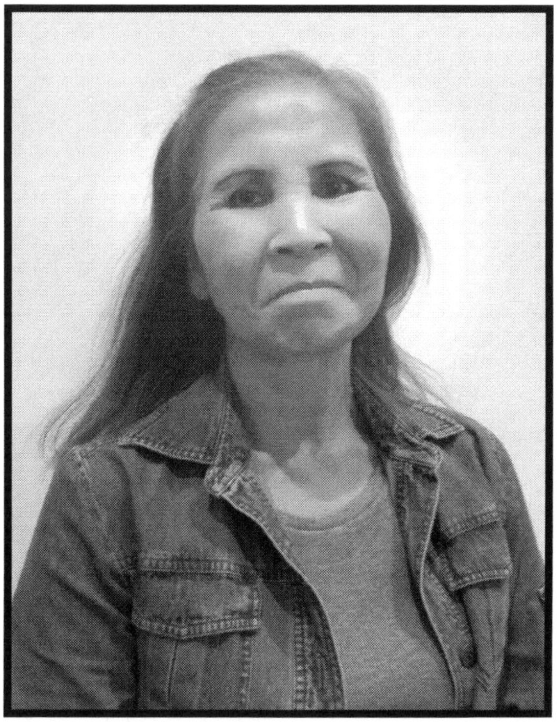

Lee – I'm from Korea

UNIT 1 – PERSONAL COMMUNICATION – LESSON 1 – INTRODUCING SELF
STUDENT BOOK PAGE 3

Continue introducing countries and eliciting conversation through questions.

Romilio – I'm from Panama

Zelda – I'm from Costa Rica

Joann – I'm from Haiti

Monica – I'm from Mexico

UNIT 1 – PERSONAL COMMUNICATION – LESSON 1 – INTRODUCING SELF
STUDENT BOOK PAGE 4

Time to Speak

A. Conversation "Hello. My Name is Shawn."

1. Ask: "Who are the 2 people in this conversation?"
2. Have students complete *To Do First* by having students repeat each line after the instructor. Repeat each line 5-6 times. Strive for a normal conversational tone rather than an oral reading tone.
3. Use backward build up for sentences longer than 4 words. Remember to divide sentences into sound units. See the Activity Bank for directions on backward build up and sound units.
4. Use correct intonation, stress, and rhythm patterns. Include the following intonation patterns:

- Statement (voice goes down at the end).
- WH-Question (voice starts high on the WH-Question word, drops in the middle of the sentence, then goes up and down on the last word.)

B. Have students complete *To Do Second* and *To Do Third*.
Call on individual student pairs to read the conversations after each Substitution has been drilled. Volunteer pairs present conversations for the class.

C. Have students complete *To Do Fourth* by introducing themselves to each other.

Time to Speak

Hello. My Name is Shawn.

1.A. Hello. My name is **Shawn.**

1.B. Hi, **Shawn.** My name is **Lee.**

2.A. So, where are you from, **Lee?**

2.B. I'm from **Korea.** What about you?

3.A. I'm from **India.**

3.B. Nice to meet you.

4.A. Nice meeting you, too.

To Do First: Repeat the conversation after the instructor.

To Do Second: Speak with a partner. Change the underlined words in the conversation for the Substitutions.

To Do Third: Change partners and repeat the Substitutions.

To Do Fourth: Change partners. Use the conversation to introduce yourselves.

Substitution No. 1

1.A. Hello. My name is **Romilio.**

1.B. Hi, **Romilio.** My name is **Zelda.**

2.A. So, where are you from, **Zelda?**

2.B. I'm from **Costa Rica.** What about you?

3.A. I'm from **Panama.**

3.B. Nice to meet you.

4.A. Nice meeting you, too.

Substitution No. 2

1.A. Hello. My name is **Joann.**

1.B. Hi, **Joann.** My name is **Monica.**

2.A. So, where are you from, **Monica?**

2.B. I'm from **Mexico.** What about you?

3.A. I'm from **Haiti.**

3.B. Nice to meet you.

4.A. Nice meeting you, too.

UNIT 1 – PERSONAL COMMUNICATION – LESSON 1 – INTRODUCING SELF
STUDENT BOOK PAGE 5

Conclude Substitution Nos. 3 and 4.

Grammar Foundation

1. Complete *To Do First* by having students read the information under The BE Verb.
2. Have students complete *To Do Second* by having students repeat each example sentence after the instructor.
3. Ask for example sentences using the structures.

Substitution No. 3

1.A. Hello. My name is **Adel.**

1.B. Hi, **Adel.** My name is **Carmen.**

2.A. So, where are you from, **Carmen?**

2.B. I'm from **Colombia.** What about you?

3.A. I'm from **Libya.**

3.B. Nice to meet you.

4.A. Nice meeting you, too.

Substitution No. 4

1.A. Hello. My name is **Nelsigleny.**

1.B. Hi, **Nelsigleny.** My name is **Gladys.**

2.A. So, where are you from, **Gladys?**

2.B. I'm from **Ecuador.** What about you?

3.A. I'm from **Venezuela.**

3.B. Nice to meet you.

4.A. Nice meeting you, too.

Grammar Foundation

The BE Verb

BE is used to describe State of Being. We use it to describe:

(1) how we are (2) who we are (3) a place we are at

How we are	Who we are	Where we are
I am sick.	I am a teacher.	I am at the library.
You are happy.	You are a student.	You are at McDonalds.
She is hungry.	She is a mother.	She is at work.
They are interesting.	They are from Ecuador.	They are in class.
We are tired.	We are from Miami.	We are at church.

UNIT 1 – PERSONAL COMMUNICATION – LESSON 1 – INTRODUCING SELF
STUDENT BOOK PAGE 6

Although it's not listed in the student text, take time to show how to make contractions with Subject + BE Verb, for example:
Affirmative Statements: I'm, he's she's, we're, you're, and they're

Negative Statements:	You're not	-or-	You aren't
	He's not	-or-	He isn't
	She's not	-or-	She isn't
	We're not	-or-	We aren't
	They're not	-or-	They aren't

Affirmative Statements

Subject + Be Verb			Subject + Be Verb		
I	am	a teacher.	You	are	a student.
He	is	well.	He	is	an uncle.
She	is	at church.	It	is	raining.
We	are	from Korea.	We	are	friends.
You	are	in Chicago.	They	are	absent.
They	are	sisters.	Romilio	is	from Panama.

To Do First: Read the information about the grammar structure.

Negative Statements

Subject + Be Verb + Not				Subject + Be Verb + Not			
I	am	not	sick.	You	are	not	a child.
She	is	not	present.	He	is	not	at the library.
It	is	not	raining.	They	are	not	from Cuba.
We	are	not	single.	You	are	not	from Libya.
They	are	not	from Miami.	She	is	not	from Colombia.

Questions

Be Verb + Subject			Answers
Are	you	happy?	Yes, I am.
Is	he	your brother?	No, he isn't.
Is	she	from Venezuela?	Yes, she is.
Is	it	raining?	No, it's not.
Are	we	in Miami?	No, we're not.
Are	you	from Haiti?	No, we aren't.
Are	they	at ESOL class?	Yes, they are.

To Do Second: Repeat the example sentences after the instructor.

UNIT 1 – PERSONAL COMMUNICATION – LESSON 1 – INTRODUCING SELF
STUDENT BOOK PAGE 7

Let's Practice

A. Conduct the Let's Practice Activity 1. What's Your Name Listening Activity

1. Instructor reads the conversation saying the word in **bold** in the brackets. Students circle the word in brackets they hear. Read each exercise 2 times.
2. Go over student responses.

Teacher answer key and transcript in bold.

1. What's your name?
   My [name's / **name**] is Barbara.
2. What's your address?
   My address [are / **is**] 2110 N.W. 152 Street.
3. [What is / **What's**] your phone number?
   My phone number is [555.435.1255 / **555.435.1222**].
4. What's your [names / **name**]?
   My [**name** / names] is Gladys Hernandez.
5. [What's / **What is**] your phone number?
   My [**phone number** / name] is 305.651.2555.
6. [**Are** / Aren't] you on Facebook?
   No I [aren't / **am**] not.
7. What [**is** / are] your e-mail address?
   I [do not / **don't**] have an e-mail address.

B. Conduct the Let's Practice Activity 2. Handling a Handshake

1. Demonstrate the culturally appropriate North American hand shake with each student. Discuss when shaking hands is appropriate. In general, in business settings, men will shake hands. For women it is optional. However, a woman herself may initiate a handshake to either a man or woman. In social settings, men should shake hands when greeting each other. For women it is optional.
2. Also discuss the importance of looking into the eyes of the person you are greeting. Explain that while in some other cultures eye contact may be considered rude, in North American culture, it is considered rude to NOT make eye contact.
3. Have students practice shaking hands with each other.

Let's Practice

1. What's Your Name Listening Activity

Listen to the conversations. Circle the word in [brackets] that you hear.

1. What's your name?

    My [name's / name] is Barbara.

2. What's your address?

    My address [are / is] 2110 N.W. 152 Street.

3. [What is / What's] your phone number?

    My phone number is [555.435.1255 / 555.435.1222].

4. What's your [names / name]?

    My [name / names] is Gladys Hernandez.

5. [What's / What is] your phone number?

    My [phone number / name] is 305.651.2555.

6. [Are / Aren't] you on Facebook?

    No I [aren't / am] not.

7. What [is / are] your e-mail address?

    I [do not / don't] have an e-mail address.

2. Handling a Handshake

The instructor will demonstrate a typical North American hand shake. Follow the instructor's directions.

UNIT 1 – PERSONAL COMMUNICATION – LESSON 1 – INTRODUCING SELF
STUDENT BOOK PAGE 8

Demonstrate the "limp fish" handshake and explain that this would be inappropriate and may send an unintended message.

C. Conduct the Let's Practice Activity 3. Interview Line-Up

1. Create two equal lines of students facing each other about 2' apart. Designate Line A and B.
2. Instructor has Line A to introduce themselves to their partners facing them in Line B.
3. When all have completed the introduction, the student at the end of Line A moves to the opposite end of Line A while other students in Line A shift one place over. Line B does NOT move. All students now face a new partner.
4. Instructor has Line B introduce themselves to their partners facing them in Line A.
5. Continue shifting Line A until all students have interviewed each other.

D. Conduct the Let's Practice Activity 4. Survey

Instructor demonstrates the survey. Ask one student the following questions and write their responses on the board:

1. What's your name?
2. Where are you from?
3. What languages do you speak?
4. Where do you live now?
5. Do you have an e-mail address?
6. Are you on Facebook?

E. Conduct the Let's Practice Activity 5. Alphabetizing Names & Countries

1. Instructor lists all students' names on the board in random order in a column titled "Name".
2. Have each student come to the board and write his/her country from next to their name under a column titled "Country From".
3. Divide into two teams. Assign one team to alphabetize the names on a piece of paper and the other team to alphabetize the countries.
4. Groups read their lists to the class.

3. Interview Line-Up

1. Make a line with other students.
2. Students will introduce themselves to each other. Follow the instructor's directions.

4. Survey

1. Talk to two classmates. Ask the questions below.
2. Write their responses on your survey.

Student 1

1. What's your name? ______________________________
2. Where are you from? ______________________________
3. What languages do you speak? ______________________________
4. Where do you live now? ______________________________
5. Do you have an e-mail address? ______________________________
6. Are you on Facebook? ______________________________

Student 2

1. What's your name? ______________________________
2. Where are you from? ______________________________
3. What languages do you speak? ______________________________
4. Where do you live now? ______________________________
5. Do you have an e-mail address? ______________________________
6. Are you on Facebook? ______________________________

5. Alphabetize Names and Countries

Work with a group. Follow the instructor's directions to alphabetize students' names and countries.

UNIT 1 – PERSONAL COMMUNICATION – LESSON 1 – INTRODUCING SELF
STUDENT BOOK PAGE 9

F. Conduct the Let's Practice Activity 6. Scrambled Spelling
NOTE: This is the Biblical Principle. **Teacher Answer Key in Bold**

1. Students work with a small group.
2. Students read the paragraph and work together to unscramble the spelling of the underlined words. Students write the word on the line next to the scrambled spelling.
3. Students read their completed paragraph to the class.
4. Instructor may wish to comment on the passage.

Moses has just met with God. God has told Moses to lead the **[people** o p p e e l ________] of Israel out of Egypt. Moses [**doesn't** d e n o s t ________] think the people will listen to him, so he asks God this [**question:** n o i t s e u q ________] "Suppose I go to the Israelites and say to them, 'The God of your [**fathers** t r a e f h s ________] has sent me to you,' and they ask me, ' [**What** h w t a ________] is his name?' Then what shall I tell them?" God said to [**Moses** s o s e m ________], "I AM WHO I AM. This is what you are to say to the [**Israelites**: s t l a s I r e i e ________] 'I AM has sent me to you.'"

Review Exercises

Assign the Review Exercises for homework. Go over the instructions to ensure students understand how to complete each activity.
Answer Key in Bold

1. Alphabetize
Alphabetize the names and countries listed in the Vocabulary in two different lists. Include:

Names: Shawn, Lee, Romilio, Zelda, Joann, Monica, Adel, Carmen, Nelsigleny, Gladys

Adel, Carmen, Gladys, Joann, Lee, Monica, Nelsigleny, Romilio, Shawn, Zelda

Countries: India, Korea, Panama, Costa Rica, Haiti, Mexico, Libya, Colombia, Venezuela, Ecuador

Colombia, Costa Rica, Ecuador, Haiti, India, Korea, Libya, Mexico, Panama, Venezuela

6. Scrambled Spelling

1. Work with a small group.
2. Read the paragraph below.
3. Unscramble the spelling of the underlined words. Write the correct word on the line.
4. Read your paragraph to the class.

Moses has just met with God. God has told Moses to lead the [o p p e e l __________] of Israel out of Egypt. Moses [d e n o s t __________] think the people will listen to him, so he asks God this [n o i t s e u q __________] "Suppose I go to the Israelites and say to them, 'The God of your [t r a e f h s __________] has sent me to you,' and they ask me, '[h w t a __________] is his name?' Then what shall I tell them?" God said to [s o s e m __________], "I AM WHO I AM. This is what you are to say to the [s t i a s l r e i e __________] 'I AM has sent me to you.'"

Review Exercises

1. Alphabetize

Alphabetize the names and countries listed in the Vocabulary in two different lists. Include:

Names: Shawn, Lee, Romilio, Zelda, Joann, Monica, Adel, Carmen, Nelsigleny, Gladys

____

____

____

Countries: India, Korea, Panama, Costa Rica, Haiti, Mexico, Libya, Colombia, Venezuela, Ecuador

____

____

____

UNIT 1 – PERSONAL COMMUNICATION – LESSON 1 – INTRODUCING SELF
STUDENT BOOK PAGE 10

2. Reading Comprehension True or False

1. Read the paragraph. Read the statements about the paragraph.
2. Circle True or False.

Teacher Answer Key in Bold

Professor Black's ESL class has ten students this semester. The students are introducing themselves to Professor Black. First is Monica. She's from Mexico. Monica has been in the U.S. for 5 years. Next is Romilio. He is from Panama. He speaks Spanish and also French. Lee is from South Korea. She speaks Korean and some Japanese, too. Zelda is from Costa Rica. She is married to Romilio. Zelda speaks Spanish and French fluently. She has been in the U.S. for 2 years. She left Panama for Canada about 20 years ago. Nelsigleny is from Venezuela. She first studied in Spain before coming to the U.S. She is a dentist in her country. Colombia is where Carmen comes from. She married an American citizen, but he died. Shawn's family comes from India. He studied to be a pharmacist. He has lived in the U.S. for 3 years. Adel was visiting from Libya when a war broke out. He couldn't get back home, so he came to ESL class. Now he likes living in the U.S. Lee married an American citizen so she has a second English teacher at home! She comes from Korea. Ecuador is the birthplace of Gladys, but she also lived in Panama. She has 3 sons so they help her with her English. Joann is from Haiti and she has studied English for just 1 year. She has progressed quickly and now has a job where she speaks English. These are the students in Professor Black's class.

True **False** 1. Professor Black has 11 students.
True False 2. Romilio is from Panama.
True **False** 3. Lee speaks Spanish and French.
True False 4. Zelda is married to Romilio.
True **False** 5. Nelsigleny was a dentist in Spain.
True **False** 6. Adel was in the war in Lybia.
True False 7. Shawn studied to be a pharmacist.
True False 8. Carmen's husband is dead.
True **False** 9. Gladys was born in Panama.
True False 10. Joann speaks English at her job.

2. Reading Comprehension True or False

1. Read the paragraph. Read the statements about the paragraph.
2. Circle True or False.

Professor Black's ESL class has ten students this semester. The students are introducing themselves to Professor Black. First is Monica. She's from Mexico. Monica has been in the U.S. for 5 years. Next is Romilio. He is from Panama. He speaks Spanish and also French. Lee is from South Korea. She speaks Korean and some Japanese, too. Zelda is from Costa Rica. She is married to Romilio. Zelda speaks Spanish and French fluently. She has been in the U.S. for 2 years. She left Panama for Canada about 20 years ago. Nelsigleny is from Venezuela. She first studied in Spain before coming to the U.S. She is a dentist in her country. Colombia is where Carmen comes from. She married an American citizen, but he died. Shawn's family comes from India. He studied to be a pharmacist. He has lived in the U.S. for 3 years. Adel was visiting from Libya when a war broke out. He couldn't get back home, so he came to ESL class. Now he likes living in the U.S. Lee married an American citizen so she has a second English teacher at home! She comes from Korea. Ecuador is the birthplace of Gladys, but she also lived in Panama. She has 3 sons so they help her with her English. Joann is from Haiti and she has studied English for just 1 year. She has progressed quickly and now has a job where she speaks English. These are the students in Professor Black's class.

True False 1. Professor Black has 11 students.

True False 2. Romilio is from Panama.

True False 3. Lee speaks Spanish and French.

True False 4. Zelda is married to Romilio.

True False 5. Nelsigleny is a dentist in Spain.

True False 6. Adel was in the war in Lybia.

True False 7. Shawn studied to be a pharmacist.

True False 8. Carmen's husband is dead.

True False 9. Gladys was born in Panama.

True False 10. Joann speaks English at her job.

UNIT 1 – PERSONAL COMMUNICATION – LESSON 2 – PHYSICAL CHARACTERISTICS STUDENT BOOK PAGE 11

A. Prayer for Students & Self

B. Lesson Objective and Functions:
- Describing physical characteristics with adjectives

C. Grammar Structures:
- Descriptive Adjectives

D. Biblical Reference or Principles:
- Isaiah 53:2b-6

E. Materials & Preparation:
- For the Let's Practice Activity 2. Color the Charicatures, either duplicate each charicature by drawing large images on the board or one each on 8 ½ x 11 papers. Alternately, direct students to draw in their books. Provide each pair of students a standard box of 8 crayons (dollar store purchase) or a variety of colored markers, or even dry erase markers if dawing the images on the board.

<u>Introduction</u>

1. When students have arrived, have them all stand up and move around the room. Ask students to closely observe and look at EVERYTHING in the room. After a minute of walking around, have students freeze in place. Then instruct them to move to the closest student and stand back to back with that student. Demonstrate standing back to back. Once all students are paired back to back, the instructor then describes from memory the student behind his/her back including hair color, sex, and clothing. Instructor then calls on one student to describe the person behind them. Continue until several or all students have described the person behind them.
2. Instructor point out the 6 charicatures, which means: a picture, description, or imitation of a person or thing in which certain striking characteristics are exaggerated in order to create a comic effect. Describe each with Descriptive Adjectives such as thin, heavy, short, tall, average height, curly hair, spiked hair, straight hair, etc.
3. Point out the difference between using HAVE for describing eyes and hair, and using BE to describe other characteristics including height and weight. For example, "Tim HAS long straight hair. He IS thin and tall."
4. Instructor describes 2 of the caricatures.
5. Ask for volunteers to describe the remaining 4 caricatures.

UNIT 1

PERSONAL COMMUNICATION

LESSON 2 – PHYSICAL CHARACTERISTICS

Top:	Tim	Paula	George
Bottom:	Rita	Mona	Jack

UNIT 1 – PERSONAL COMMUNICATION – LESSON 2 – PHYSICAL CHARACTERISTICS
STUDENT BOOK PAGE 12

Introduce New Vocabulary
Have students open to Unit 1 Personal Communication; Lesson 2 Physical Characteristics. Introduce the words or phrases with a repetition drill. For instruction on conducting repetition drills, see Activity Bank. Repeat each 5-6 times.
Elicit conversation by asking questions such as:

- What is your favorite actress or actor's name?
- What is your opinion of men wearing long hair?
- Do you watch American football?
- What other sports do you enjoy?
- Do you know anyone who has dreadlocks?
- How long have they grown their dreadlocks?"

actress

long straight hair

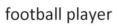

football player

dreadlocks

UNIT 1 – PERSONAL COMMUNICATION – LESSON 2 – PHYSICAL CHARACTERISTICS
STUDENT BOOK PAGE 13

Continue introducing words and phrases with repetition drill.
Continue eliciting conversation with questions such as:

- Do you like rock music? Why or why not?
- Do you know anyone with spiked hair? How do they take care of their hair?
- Who is a favorite professor you have had in the past? Tell why they were your favorite.
- Do you prefer curly or straight hair? Why?

rock guitarist

spiked hair

professor

curly hair

UNIT 1 – PERSONAL COMMUNICATION – LESSON 2 – PHYSICAL CHARACTERISTICS
STUDENT BOOK PAGE 14

Continue introducing words and phrases with repetition drill.
Continue eliciting conversation with questions such as:

- What do you think when you see someone smiling?
- Who do you know with large muscles? How did they get their large muscles?
- What is your opinion about tattoos? Do you have a tattoo?
- What do you think about the message of this tattoo? What does it mean 'created by God?'
- Do children wearing glasses get teased in your country? How are they teased? What is said?

sweet smile

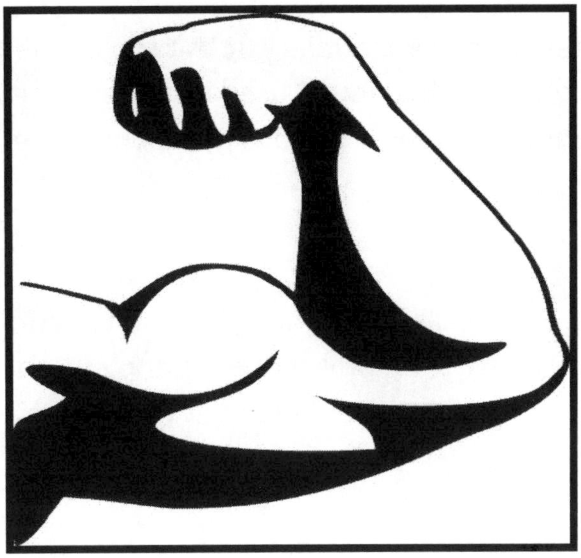

rippling muscles

tattoo

glasses

UNIT 1 – PERSONAL COMMUNICATION – LESSON 2 – PHYSICAL CHARACTERISTICS
STUDENT BOOK PAGE 15

Review the vocabulary at the top of the page in the box.
Point out the Nouns used as idiomatic expressions: "a hunk; a looker." Ensure students understand and can use this terminology.

Time to Speak

A. Conversation Who's Bridget Beautiful?
   1. Ask: "Who are the 2 people in this conversation?"
   2. Have students complete *To Do First* by having students repeat each line after the instructor. Repeat each line 5-6 times. Strive for a normal conversational tone rather than an oral reading tone.
   3. Use backward build up for sentences longer than 4 words. Remember to divide sentences into sound units. See the Activity Bank for directions on backward build up and sound units.
   4. Use correct intonation, stress, and rhythm patterns. Include the following intonation patterns:
   - Statement (voice goes down at the end).
   - WH-Question (voice starts high on the WH-Question word, drops in the middle of the sentence, then goes up and down on the last word.)

B. Have students complete *To Do Second* and *To Do Third*.
Call on individual student pairs to read the conversations after each Substitution has been drilled. Volunteer pairs present conversations for the class.

People	Adjectives for Hair	Adjectives	Nouns	
actress	curly		dreadlocks	smile
football player	long	rippling	glasses	tattoo
professor	short	sweet	muscles	a hunk
rock guitarist	spiked			a looker
	straight	hot		

Time to Speak

Who's Bridget Beautiful?

1.A. I like **Bridget Beautiful**.

1.B. Who's **Bridget Beautiful**?

2.A. You know, she's that **actress** with the **long straight hair.**

2.B. Oh, you mean the one with the **sweet smile?**

3.A. That's the one.

3.B. You're right. **She's a looker**!

Substitution No. 1

1.A. I like **John Eskridge**.

1.B. Who's **John Eskridge**?

2.A. You know, he's that **football player** with the **long dreadlocks.**

2.B. Oh, you mean the one with the **rippling muscles?**

3.A. That's the one.

To Do First: Repeat the conversation after the instructor.

To Do Second: Speak with a partner. Change the underlined words in the conversation for the Substitutions.

To Do Third: Change partners and repeat the Substitutions.

UNIT 1 – PERSONAL COMMUNICATION – LESSON 2 – PHYSICAL CHARACTERISTICS
STUDENT BOOK PAGE 16

Conclude the Substitution Nos. 2 and 3.

Grammar Foundation

1. Complete *To Do First* by having students read the information under Descriptive Adjectives.
2. Have students complete *To Do Second* by having students repeat each example sentence after the instructor.
3. Ask for example sentences using the structures.

3.B. You're right. **He's a hunk**!

Substitution No. 2

1.A. I like **Rock Rodman**.

1.B. Who's **Rock Rodman**?

2.A. You know, he's that **rock guitarist** with the **spiked hair.**

2.B. Oh, you mean the one with the **tattoo?**

3.A. That's the one.

3.B. You're right. **He's hot**!

Substitution No. 3

1.A. I like **Professor Newman**.

1.B. Who's **Professor Newman**?

2.A. You know, she's that **speech professor** with the **short curly hair.**

2.B. Oh, you mean the one with the **glasses?**

3.A. That's the one.

3.B. You're right. **She's sweet**!

Grammar Foundation

Descriptive Adjectives

Descriptive Adjectives are used to describe nouns or pronouns: persons, places, things.
Adjectives come before nouns in the normal English word order.
Adjectives change or modify the meaning of the noun a little.
Adjectives come in front of the noun they modify.
For example:

	Adjective + Noun	
I am a	rock	guitarist.
You have	rippling	muscles.
He has	spiked	hair.

To Do First: Read the information about the grammar structure.

To Do Second: Repeat the example sentences after the instructor.

UNIT 1 – PERSONAL COMMUNICATION – LESSON 2 – PHYSICAL CHARACTERISTICS
STUDENT BOOK PAGE 17

Conclude the Grammar Foundation BE + Adjective and Contraction + Adjective.

<u>Let's Practice</u>

<u>A. Conduct the Let's Practice Activity 1. Listening Activity</u>
Instructor reads the passage at a normal pace. Students circle the words they hear in the [brackets].
Ensure students you will read all the way through as often as students request. It is not uncommon to read 4 or more times. This is 'real world' listening at the pace of normal conversation.
Note the **Teacher Answer Key and Transcript in Bold.** Read the word in **bold.**

When finished, have students read the paragraph to check responses. Ask for volunteers to each read a couple of sentences.

Have students review the passage and count the number of new students mentioned.

Professor Black is describing the students in her ESL class to her husband. "I have [**several** / many] new students this semester. First, there's Monica. She has a [**sweet** / short] smile. Juan is a body builder and he has [ripped / **rippling**] muscles. He also has a [tattoos / **tattoo**] on his arm which says, 'created by God.' I asked him what that means and he told me that he was created by God. He said that he did not descend from a monkey. I've also got a math professor in the class. He has [**spiked** / spice] hair. Then there's the football player named Conner. He has [dreadlocks / **curly**] hair under his helmet. Vanessa is from Cuba. She was an [**actress** / actor] before she came to the U.S. She has [**glasses** / glass] and very long [**straight** / tall] hair. So, how many new students did I describe?" asked Professor Black. "I can't remember," replied Mr. Black. So, why don't you count them? Write the total number of new students here: <u>**5**</u> .

She has a	sweet	smile.
He has	long	dreadlocks.

When using the BE Verb with an Adjective, the Adjective comes after the BE Verb. For example:

	Be Verb + Adjective	
I	am	happy.
You	are	handsome.
He	is	old.
She	is	beautiful.
We	are	hungry.
They	are	young.

The BE VERB is often contracted with the pronoun. For example:

Contraction + Adjective	
He's	hot.
She's	sweet.
They're	smart.

Let's Practice

1. Listening Activity

1. Listen to the instructor read the passage. Circle the word [in brackets] that you hear.
2. Go over responses with the class.

Professor Black is describing the students in her ESL class to her husband. "I have [several / many] new students this semester. First, there's Monica. She has a [sweet / short] smile. Juan is a body builder and he has [ripped / rippling] muscles. He also has a [tattoos / tattoo] on his arm which says, 'created by God.' I asked him what that means and he told me that he was created by God. He said that he did not descend from a monkey. I've also got a math professor in the class. He has [spiked / spice] hair. Then there's the football player named Conner. He has [dreadlocks / curly] hair under his helmet. Vanessa is from Cuba. She was an [actress / actor] before she came to the U.S. She has [glasses / glass] and very long [straight / tall] hair. So, how many new students did I describe?" asked Professor Black. "I can't remember," replied Mr. Black. So, why don't you count them? Write the total number of new students here: ________________.

UNIT 1 – PERSONAL COMMUNICATION – LESSON 2 – PHYSICAL CHARACTERISTICS
STUDENT BOOK PAGE 18

B. Conduct the Let's Practice Activity 2. Color the Caricatures

1. See note under Materials & Preparation. Have students color the caricatures per your selected method.
2. Give instructions such as:
   - "Tim has brown hair." Students respond by coloring Tim's hair brown.
   - "Tim has a red shirt and blue pants." Students color Tim's shirt red and his pants blue.
3. Continue giving instructions using HAVE and BE verbs accordingly until all of your chosen caricatures are colored.

C. Conduct the Let's Practice Activity 3. Mystery Person

- Use the colored caricatures produced in the previous activity.
- The instructor thinks about one of the caricatures, for example, Tim.
- Students ask questions to discover which caricature the instructor is thinking about.
- Instructor can only answer questions with YES or NO.
- Ensure students understand how to ask a YES/NO question. For example, the instructor cannot answer with YES or NO the question, "Is this caricature a man or woman?"
- Once a student thinks they know the caricature the instructor is thinking about, they may guess. If correct, they get a point. If incorrect, they are out and cannot ask any further questions.
- Encourage asking questions to discover the caricature's identify. Discourage the repeated question, "Is it Tim? Is it Paula? Is it George?" etc. The point is to formulate questions and deduce the answer from the information gathered.

D. Conduct the Let's Practice Activity 4. Reading for Information

1. Instructor reads the passage while students follow along silently.
2. After reading each section 2 times, the instructor asks questions about the passage. See the questions following each section.
3. When finished, lead students to read the passage a section at a time after the instructor.
4. NOTE: This is the Biblical principle. Instructor may wish to comment on the passage from Isaiah 53:2b-6.

2. Color the Caricatures

Follow the instructor's directions to color the caricatures.

3. Mystery Person

1. The instructor will think about one of the caricatures. Students ask questions to discover which caricature the instructor is thinking about.
2. The instructor can only answer the questions with YES or NO. Ask questions, for example: "Is this caricature a man?" The instructor can answer YES or NO. Do NOT ask questions, for example: "Is this caricature a man or woman?" The instructor cannot answer only with YES or NO to this kind of question.
3. When you think you know which caricature the instructor is thinking about, you may ask, for example: "Is it Tim?" If you are correct, you get a point. If you are incorrect, you are out and may not ask any more questions.

4. Reading for Information

1. The instructor will read the passage. Follow along silently.
2. After reading a short time, the instructor will ask questions about the passage.
3. Read the passage after the instructor.

a. He had no special beauty or form to make us notice him.
b. There was nothing in his appearance to make us desire him.
c. He was hated and rejected by people.
d. He had much pain and suffering.
e. People would not even look at him.
f. He was hated, and we didn't even notice him.
g. But he took our suffering on him and felt our pain for us.
h. We saw his suffering.
i. We thought God was punishing him.
j. But he was wounded for the wrong things we did.
k. He was crushed for the evil things we did.
l. The punishment, which made us well, was given to him.
m. And we are healed because of his wounds.
n. We all have wandered away like sheep.
o. Each of us has gone his own way.
p. But the Lord has put on him the punishment for all the evil we have done.

UNIT 1 – PERSONAL COMMUNICATION – LESSON 2 – PHYSICAL CHARACTERISTICS
STUDENT BOOK PAGE 19

a. He had no special beauty or form to make us notice him.
b. There was nothing in his appearance to make us desire him.
   - T/**F** He was beautiful.
c. He was hated and rejected by people.
d. He had much pain and suffering.
   - **T**/F People hated him.
e. People would not even look at him.
f. He was hated, and we didn't even notice him.
   - T/**F** Everyone loved him.
g. But he took our suffering on him and felt our pain for us.
h. We saw his suffering.
   - **T**/F He felt our pain.
i. We thought God was punishing him.
j. But he was wounded for the wrong things we did.
   - T/**F** God was punishing him.
k. He was crushed for the evil things we did.
l. The punishment, which made us well, was given to him.
   - **T**/F The punishment made us well.
m. And we are healed because of his wounds.
n. We all have wandered away like sheep.
   - **T**/F The passage says we are like sheep.
o. Each of us has gone his own way.
p. But the Lord has put on him the punishment for all the evil we have done.
   - **T**/F The Lord put our punishment on him.

Review Exercises

Assign the Review Exercises for homework. Go over the instructions to ensure students understand how to complete each activity. **Answer Key in Bold**

2. Correct the Mistakes

Students find the mistakes and write the corrected sentence on the line.

1. The actress have long straight hair. ***The actress HAS long straight hair.***
2. George be heavy and tall. **George is heavy and tall.**

Review Exercises

1. Write a Paragraph

Write a paragraph 6-8 sentences. Describe the caricatures in the book: Tim, Paula, George, Rita, Mona, and Jack. Use the verbs HAVE and BE. For example:

Tim has brown hair. He is tall and thin. He has a red shirt and blue pants.

2. Correct the Mistakes

1. Each sentence has some mistakes.
2. Correct the mistakes.
3. Write the correct sentence on the line.

1. The actress have long straight hair. ***The actress HAS long straight hair.***
2. George be heavy and tall.
3. She wear glasses and have curly hair.
4. Ron has dreadlock.
5. Juan's tattoos says 'created by God.'
6. Becky like rippling muscle on men.
7. The rock guitarist has spike hair.
8. The football players has number 44 shirt.
9. Tina have short and thin.
10. Jack be spiked hair.

UNIT 1 – PERSONAL COMMUNICATION – LESSON 2 – PHYSICAL CHARACTERISTICS
STUDENT BOOK PAGE 20

3. Hidden Word Puzzle

Circle the hidden words in the puzzle. **Teacher answer key in *bold italic.***

PROFESSOR	ACTRESS	GUITARIST	DREADLOCKS	RIPPLING
CURLY	SPIKED	GLASSES	TATTOO	HUNK
BEAUTIFUL	SWEET			

N	K	H	K	E	W	O	J	E	S	***P***	***R***	***O***	***F***	***E***	***S***	***S***	***O***	***R***	A	T	U	S	N	K	L	Q	I	U	W	E	O
P	Y	U	B	V	C	X	P	A	S	D	F	G	H	K	L	N	M	B	***H***	***U***	***N***	***K***	S	D	F	G	S	A	P	Q	I
D	N	I	***B***	***E***	***A***	***U***	***T***	***I***	***F***	***U***	***L***	U	Y	T	R	E	W	Q	K	L	K	J	H	H	G	F	D	S	S	A	W
N	T	O	N	M	B	V	C	X	D	E	N	I	O	***R***	***I***	***P***	***P***	***L***	***I***	***N***	***G***	N	W	T	Q	J	T	H	E	M	N
I	O	P	W	N	J	N	***C***	***U***	***R***	***L***	***Y***	K	L	N	I	N	E	T	N	E	L	N	D	G	N	X	T	C	X	T	T
R	M	N	N	I	O	P	Y	T	N	B	G	F	M	I	V	Y	F	A	G	E	W	***S***	***W***	***E***	***E***	***T***	Q	U	Y	T	R
N	B	J	A	S	M	J	F	A	T	U	N	H	E	R	N	K	O	Q	W	N	K	T	N	A	N	K	E	W	Q	O	U
B	R	***T***	***A***	***T***	***T***	***O***	***O***	N	I	Q	W	N	E	I	B	T	E	W	Q	I	Y	W	I	C	X	S	I	N	Q	W	E
R	R	B	N	V	C	Q	***A***	***C***	***T***	***R***	***E***	***S***	***S***	N	I	Y	T	R	E	Q	N	I	O	N	W	T	A	L	O	H	W
A	N	Y	S	N	I	Y	I	O	W	T	N	Q	I	O	U	Y	T	H	N	K	A	T	N	N	I	U	Y	E	N	M	L
W	O	N	T	E	W	Q	N	V	J	A	L	***D***	***R***	***E***	***A***	***D***	***L***	***O***	***C***	***K***	***S***	N	Q	W	E	R	T	Y	I	O	P
N	K	H	***S***	***P***	***I***	***K***	***E***	***D***	G	E	N	H	H	A	Z	I	S	W	T	I	Y	N	I	W	T	R	W	O	R	K	N
N	T	N	N	I	I	O	Y	Y	I	I	N	I	E	T	G	D	A	B	N	I	N	E	N	B	X	O	N	Q	W	E	R
T	F	R	D	E	W	B	N	I	N	O	I	N	O	T	E	N	I	W	O	T	O	A	S	V	T	N	I	N	K	H	I
Y	E	N	S	T	T	H	I	***G***	***U***	***I***	***T***	***A***	***R***	***I***	***S***	***T***	M	E	S	Q	W	E	R	T	Y	U	I	O	B	M	T
T	***G***	***L***	***A***	***S***	***S***	***E***	***S***	T	N	I	N	D	A	L	S	Y	N	I	Y	R	T	W	Q	N	M	B	X	B	F	V	T

3. Hidden Word Puzzle

Circle the words in the puzzle.

PROFESSOR	ACTRESS	GUITARIST	DREADLOCKS	RIPPLING
CURLY	SPIKED	GLASSES	TATTOO	HUNK
BEAUTIFUL	SWEET			

```
N K H K E W O J E S P R O F E S S O R A T U S N K L Q I U W E O
P Y U B V C X P A S D F G H K L N M B H U N K S D F G S A P Q I
D N I B E A U T I F U L U Y T R E W Q K L K J H H G F D S S A W
N T O N M B V C X D E N I O R I P P L I N G N W T Q J T H E M N
I O P W N J N C U R L Y K L N I N E T N E L N D G N X T C X T T
R M N N I O P Y T N B G F M I V Y F A G E W S W E E T Q U Y T R
N B J A S M J F A T U N H E R N K O Q W N K T N A N K E W Q O U
B R T A T T O O N I Q W N E I B T E W Q I Y W I C X S I N Q W E
R R B N V C Q A C T R E S S N I Y T R E Q N I O N W T A L O H W
A N Y S N I Y I O W T N Q I O U Y T H N K A T N N I U Y E N M L
W O N T E W Q N V J A L D R E A D L O C K S N Q W E R T Y I O P
N K H S P I K E D G E N H H A Z I S W T I Y N I W T R W O R K N
N T N N I I O Y Y I I N I E T G D A B N I N E N B X O N Q W E R
T F R D E W B N I N O I N O T E N I W O T O A S V T N I N K H I
Y E N S T T H I G U I T A R I S T M E S Q W E R T Y U I O B M T
T G L A S S E S T N I N D A L S Y N I Y R T W Q N M B X B V W T
```

UNIT 2 – THE COMMUNITY – LESSON 1 – 911 EMERGENCY!
STUDENT BOOK PAGE 21

A. Prayer for Students & Self

B. Lesson Objective and Functions:
- Reporting emergencies to 911

C. Grammar Structures:
- Present Progressive Tense

D. Biblical Reference or Principles:
- God is always with his children

E. Materials & Preparation:
1. For the Let's Practice Activity 2. Emergency Concentration – Matching Activity prepare a Concentration game board following instructions in the Activity Bank.
2. Also prepare the card matches as described in B. Conduct the Let's Practice Activity 2. Emergency Concentration.

<u>Introduction</u>

1. Instructor tells any stories he/she may know about calling 911.
2. If unable to think of a story, use the following:
3. While teaching the lesson on calling 911, the author taught students to whisper when calling 911 if there was a burglar in the house. The next day, a student returned to class and reported that when she had gone home after the 911 lesson, a burglar broke into her home while she was inside. She immediately hid herself in a closet, took her cell phone, and called 911, whispering that there was a burglar in the house. The operator sent the police which arrived as the burglar was assaulting her. The burglar ran away and the police were able to catch him. The student had a black eye and bruises on her arms in witness of her ordeal.
4. Say: "This is the reason we are having this lesson today on calling 911 for an emergency."
5. Point out the vocabulary box, but don't teach it from this page.

UNIT 2
THE COMMUNITY

LESSON 1 – 911 EMERGENCY!

Need Help Now?
Stop and Call:

911

Nouns		Verbs	Adjectives
address	house	breathe – breathing – breathed	hurt
ambulance	police	call – calling – called	
burglar	purse	steal – stealing – stole	
car accident			
child			

UNIT 2 – THE COMMUNITY – LESSON 1 – 911 EMERGENCY!
STUDENT BOOK PAGE 22

Introduce New Vocabulary

Have students open to Unit 2 – The Community; Lesson 1 – 911 Emergency!
Introduce the words or phrases with a repetition drill. For instruction on conducting repetition drills, see Activity Bank. Repeat each 5-6 times.
Elicit conversation by asking questions about the pictures, for example:

- Have you ever had a burglar in your house? What happened?
- Have you ever had to call the police? Why?

burglar

house

call the Police at 911

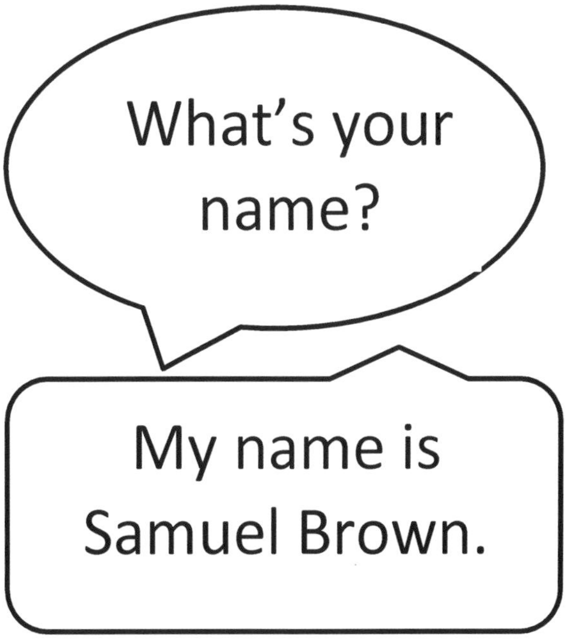

What’s your name?
My name is Samuel Brown.

UNIT 2 – THE COMMUNITY – LESSON 1 – 911 EMERGENCY!
STUDENT BOOK PAGE 23

Continue introducing vocabulary words and phrases and eliciting conversation through questions.

What's your address?

12755 S.W. 20 Street, Miramar

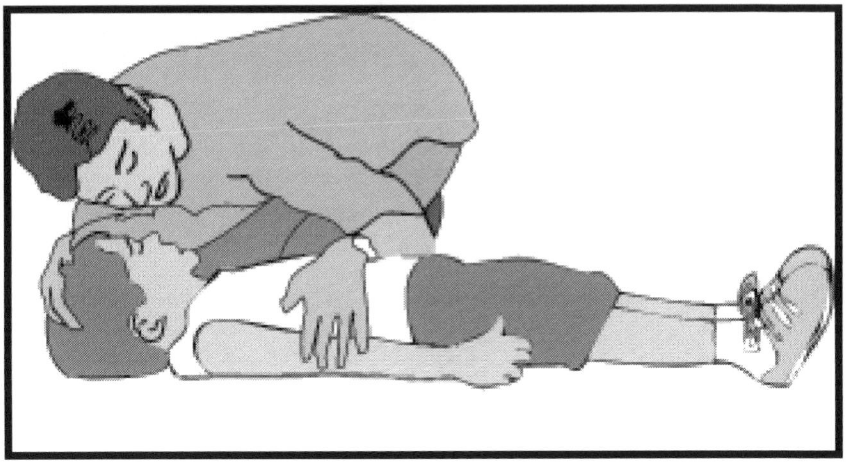

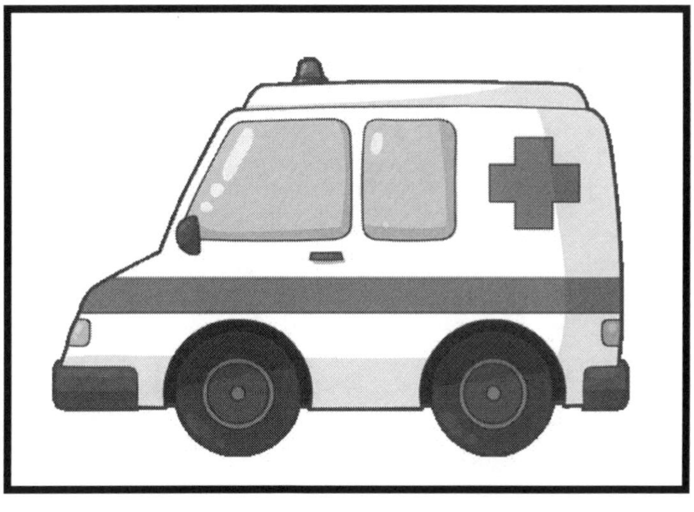

Top: The child fell into the pool.

Above: The child isn't breathing so call 911.

Right: ambulance

UNIT 2 – THE COMMUNITY – LESSON 1 – 911 EMERGENCY!
STUDENT BOOK PAGE 24

Continue introducing vocabulary words and phrases and eliciting conversation through questions.

The man stole the woman's purse so call 911.

There's a car accident so call 911.

UNIT 2 – THE COMMUNITY – LESSON 1 – 911 EMERGENCY!
STUDENT BOOK PAGE 25

Time to Speak

A. Conversation 911 Emergency!

1. Ask: "Who are the 2 people in this conversation?"
2. Have students complete *To Do First* by having students repeat each line after the instructor. Repeat each line 5-6 times. Strive for a normal conversational tone rather than an oral reading tone.
3. Use backward build up for sentences longer than 4 words. Remember to divide sentences into sound units. See the Activity Bank for directions on backward build up and sound units.
4. Use correct intonation, stress, and rhythm patterns. Include the following intonation patterns:

- Statement (voice goes down at the end).
- WH-Question (voice starts high on the WH-Question word, drops in the middle of the sentence, then goes up and down on the last word.)
- YES/NO Question (voice goes up on the end).

B. Have students complete *To Do Second* and *To Do Third*.
Call on individual student pairs to read the conversations after each Substitution has been drilled. Volunteer pairs present conversations for the class.

Time to Speak

911 Emergency!

1.A. 911 Emergency.

1.B. **There's a burglar in my house**!

2.A. **Has the burglar seen you**?

2.B. No!

3.A. I'm sending **the police** right away. What's your name?

3.B. **Samuel Brown.**

4.A. What's your address?

4.B. **4290 S.W. 30 Street, Hollywood**.

4.B. What's your phone number?

5.B. **555.983.1789**.

To Do First: Repeat the conversation after the instructor.

To Do Second: Speak with a partner. Change the underlined words in the conversation for the Substitutions.

To Do Third: Change partners and repeat the Substitutions.

Substitution No. 1

1.A. 911 Emergency.

1.B. **A child fell into the swimming pool**!

2.A. **Is he breathing**?

2.B. No!

3.A. I'm sending **an ambulance** right way.

What's your name?

3.B. **Gloria Green**.

4.A. What's your address?

4.B. **12755 S.W. 20 Street, Miramar**.

5.B. What's your phone number?

5.B. **555.322.4399**.

UNIT 2 – THE COMMUNITY – LESSON 1 – 911 EMERGENCY!
STUDENT BOOK PAGE 26

Conclude Substitution Nos. 2 and 3.

Pair students. Have them ask the question in the box below. Student volunteers share their responses with the class.

Substitution No. 2

1.A. 911 Emergency.

1.B. **A man attacked a woman and stole her purse!**

2.A. **Is she hurt?**

2.B. Yes!

3.A. I'm sending **the police** right away. What's your name?

3.B. **Della Smith.**

4.A. What's your address?

4.B. **1569 N.W. 93 Avenue, Pembroke Pines.**

5.A. What's your phone number?

5.B. **555.704.4980.**

Substitution No. 3

1.A. 911 Emergency

1.B. **There's an accident on the corner of Palm and Johnson!**

2.A. **Is anyone hurt**?

2.B. Yes!

3.A. I'm sending **an ambulance** right away. What's your name?

3.B. **John Rodriguez**.

4.A. What's your address?

4.B. **12554 Cove Road, Cooper City**.

5.A. What's your phone number?

5.B. **555.434.9881.**

Talk with a partner. Ask the question: How do people get help in an emergency in your country? Do they call the police or call a neighbor or friend for help?

UNIT 2 – THE COMMUNITY – LESSON 1 – 911 EMERGENCY!
STUDENT BOOK PAGE 27

Grammar Foundation

1. Complete *To Do First* by having students read the information under Present Progressive Tense.
2. Have students complete *To Do Second* by having students repeat each example sentence after the instructor.
3. Ask for example sentences using the structures.

Grammar Foundation

Present Progressive Tense

Present Progressive Tense is also known as Present Continuous Tense. We use the Present Progressive Tense to describe action that is happening at the present moment. It is continuous action. It is action that is happening while the speaker is speaking.

Affirmative Statements

Subject + Be Verb + Main Verb + 'Ing Ending

I	am	walking.
You	are	talking to the 911 operator.
He	is	eating.
I	am	sending an ambulance.
She	is	calling the police.
We	are	helping a hurt woman.
They	are	reading their books.

To Do First: Read the information about the grammar structure.

To Do Second: Repeat the example sentences after the instructor.

Negative Statements

Subject + Be Verb + Not Main Verb + 'Ing Ending

I	am	not	giving my phone number.
You	are	not	calling the police.
He	is	not	moving.
She	is	not	calling 911
The child	is	not	breathing.
We	are	not	walking.
They	are	not	eating.

UNIT 2 – THE COMMUNITY – LESSON 1 – 911 EMERGENCY!
STUDENT BOOK PAGE 28

Continue introducing the Questions format and reading the example sentences.

Direct students to complete the sentences. Do exercise Nos. 1-4 together and go over responses. Assign Nos. 5-12 for homework.

Answer Key - Answers in Bold

1. (send) The 911 Operator **is sending** an ambulance now.
2. (breathe, not) The **child is not breathing** now.
3. (call) The woman **is calling** 911 Emergency.
4. (attack) A man **is attacking** a woman now.
5. (watch) I **am watching** TV now.
6. (eat, not) You **are not eating** chicken tonight.
7. (drink) They **are drinking** Coca Cola now.
8. (send) The 911 Operator **is calling** the police.
9. (rain) **Is** it **raining** outside right now?
10. (call) **Are** you **calling** 911?
11. (eat) **Is** she **eating** dinner with us?
12. (speak) **Are** they **speaking** to the teacher now?

Questions

Question Word +	Be Verb +	Subject +	Main Verb + 'Ing Ending	Answer
	Are	you	calling the police?	Yes, I am.
	Is	she	sending an ambulance?	No, she isn't.
When	are	you	eating breakfast?	In the morning.
Why	is	she	crying?	Because a man attacked her.
	Are	they	calling 911?	Yes, they are.
	Are	you	swimming?	No, we aren't.
Where	are	you	going?	We're going home.
Why	are	you	calling 911?	We had an accident.

Complete the sentences. Use the verbs in parentheses.

Example: (walk) John ***is walking*** ___ to work right now.

1. (send) The 911 Operator__________________________ an ambulance now.
2. (breathe, not) The child _____________________________________ now.
3. (call) The woman ________________________________ 911 Emergency.
4. (attack) A man ____ a woman now.
5. (watch) I __________________________________ TV now.
6. (eat, not) You ___________________________________chicken tonight.
7. (drink) They _____________________________________Coca Cola now.
8. (send) The 911 Operator ____________________________________ the police.
9. (rain) ________ it ____________________ outside right now?
10. (call) ________ you _________________ 911?
11. (eat) ________ she _________________dinner with us?
12. (speak) ______ they _________________ to the teacher now?

UNIT 2 – THE COMMUNITY – LESSON 1 – 911 EMERGENCY!
STUDENT BOOK PAGE 29

Let's Practice

A. Conduct the Let's Practice Activity 1. What's the Next Line?

Students circle the correct response to each statement. **Teacher Answer Key in Bold**

1. A man attacked me in C. B. Smith Park!

A: Are you hurt? B. He ran away.

2. A child fell into the swimming pool!

A: Is he swimming? **B. Is he breathing?**

3. There's a burglar in my house!

A: Has the burglar seen you? B. What time is it?

4. There's an accident on I-75 at Griffin Road!

A: Is anyone hurt? B. I'm calling an ambulance.

5. What's your name?

A: My name is Barbara. B. I don't know.

6. What's your address?

A: I live in Panama. **B. My address is 198 Flamingo Road, Pembroke Pines, FL.**

7. What's your phone number?

A: **My phone number is 555-222-1111**. B. I left my phone at home.

Let's Practice

1. What's the Next Line?

Read the statements. You will find two responses. Circle the correct response.

1. A man attacked me in C. B. Smith Park!

A: Are you hurt? B. He ran away.

2. A child fell into the swimming pool!

A: Is he swimming? B. Is he breathing?

3. There's a burglar in my house!

A: Has the burglar seen you? B. What time is it?

4. There's an accident on I-75 at Griffin Road!

A: Is anyone hurt? B. I'm calling an ambulance.

5. What's your name?

A: My name is Barbara. B. I don't know.

6. What's your address?

A: I live in Panama. B. My address is 198 Flamingo Road, Pembroke Pines, FL.

7. What's your phone number?

A: My phone number is 555-222-1111. B. I left my phone at home.

UNIT 2 – THE COMMUNITY – LESSON 1 – 911 EMERGENCY!
STUDENT BOOK PAGE 30

B. Conduct the Let's Practice Activity 2. Emergency Concentration – Matching

For instructions on how to prepare a Concentration game board and how to play Concentration, see Activity Bank.

Prepare in advance the Concentration 3x5 cards using the emergencies and operator responses from the dialogue and substitutions including the following matches:

Emergency	Operator Responses
A man attacked me in the park!	Are you hurt?
There's a burglar in my house!	Has the burglar seen you?
There's an accident on I-75 at Griffin Road.	Is anyone hurt?
A child fell into the swimming pool!	Is he breathing?

C. Conduct the Let's Practice Activity 3. Emergency Role Play

1. Pair students.
2. Assign each pair one of the role plays in the boxes.
3. Give a few minutes for partners to practice their role plays.
4. Student pairs present their role plays to the class.

2. Emergency Concentration - Matching Activity

1. Work with a partner or work with the whole class.
2. In the Concentration game board are some cards. Half of the cards have emergencies and the other half of the cards have 911 operator responses. For example: There's a car accident! = Is anyone hurt?
3. Student 1 chooses 2 cards from the Concentration board and reads them to the class. If the 2 cards match – they are removed from the board and Student 1 receives one point.
4. Student 2 chooses 2 cards from the Concentration board and reads them to the class. If the 2 cards do NOT match – Student 2 puts these cards back into the board.
5. Continue until all cards are matched and removed from the board.

3. Emergency Role Play

1. Work with a partner. The instructor will assign each pair of students one of the role plays in the boxes below. Student 1 is the Caller. Student 2 is the 911 Operator.
2. Partners practice their role plays. Partners present their role plays to the class.

Your child fell into the swimming pool and is not breathing.	There's an accident on Pines Boulevard.	There's a burglar taking your bicycle.
1	2	3
A man in a restaurant is not breathing.	A man attacked you and took your bag.	
4	5	

UNIT 2 – THE COMMUNITY – LESSON 1 – 911 EMERGENCY!
STUDENT BOOK PAGE 31

D. Conduct the Let's Practice Activity 4. Play Beat the Cat

1. For instructions on preparing and playing Beat the Cat, see Activity Bank.
2. Use this puzzle sentence: "God is always with his children."
3. NOTE: This is the Biblical Principal. Instructor may wish to comment on the sentence.

Review Exercises

Assign the Review Exercises for homework. Go over the instructions to ensure students understand how to complete each activity.
Answer Key in Bold

1. Put the Conversation in Order

Students number the lines of the conversation into correct order.

____**4**____ You call 911. I'll get the restaurant manager.
____**1**____Oh, no! That man isn't breathing.
____**2**____ How do you know he isn't breathing?
____**3**____ He's holding his throat. What should we do?
____**6**____ Good. I'm going to find the restaurant manager.
____**5**____ O.K. I'm calling 911 right now.

2. Mystery Word Search Puzzle

1. Students complete the sentences using clues in the Conversation and Substitutions 911 Emergency!
2. Students write the answers from the sentences on the lines in the puzzle—one letter on each line.
3. When finished, a mystery word will appear inside the box.
4. Write the mystery word on the line.

4. Play Beat the Cat

1. This game is like the TV show Wheel of Fortune. The instructor will put a puzzle on the board.
2. Students take turns guessing consonants.
3. If the consonant is in the puzzle, the instructor will write it on the line. If the consonant is NOT in the puzzle, the instructor will draw part of a cat.
4. Continue until only vowels are left in the puzzle.

Review Exercises

1. Put the Conversation in Order

You will see the lines of a conversation. They are not in correct order.
Number the order of the lines of the conversation.

__________ You call 911. I'll get the restaurant manager.

____**1**____ Oh, no! That man isn't breathing.

__________ How do you know he isn't breathing?

__________ He's holding his throat. What should we do?

__________ Good. I'm going to find the restaurant manager.

__________ O.K. I'm calling 911 right now.

2. Mystery Word Search Puzzle

1. Complete the sentences below. For clues, see the Conversation and Substitutions 911 Emergency!
2. Write the answers from the sentences on the lines in the puzzle. Put one letter on each line.
3. When finished, a mystery word will appear inside the box.
4. Write the mystery word on the line.

UNIT 2 – THE COMMUNITY – LESSON 1 – 911 EMERGENCY!
STUDENT BOOK PAGE 32

1. My sons went swimming at the **pool**.
2. Yesterday I bought a new cell **phone**.
3. The instructor taught us to whisper when calling 911 if there is a **burglar** in the house.
4. A man in a restaurant is holding his throat and he is not **breathing**.
5. There's an accident on the **corner** of Pines Boulevard and Flamingo Road.
6. "911. Is this an **emergency**?"

1.							p	o	o	l		
2.					p	**h**	o	n	e			
3.			b	u	r	g	l	a	r			
4.	b	r	e	a	t	h	i	n	g			
5.							c	o	r	n	e	r
6.		e	m	e	r	g	e	n	c	y		

A mystery word will appear inside the box. Write it here: **police**

1. My sons went swimming at the ______*pool*______.
2. Yesterday I bought a new cell _______________.
3. The instructor taught us to whisper when calling 911 if there is a _______________ in the house.
4. A man in a restaurant is holding his throat and he is not _______________.
5. There's an accident on the _______________ of Pines Boulevard and Flamingo Road.
6. "911. Is this an _______________?"

```
1.                |p|o o l
2.            _ _ |_|_ _
3.        _ _ _ _ |_|_ _
4.    _ _ _ _ _ _ |_|_ _
5.                |_|_ _ _ _ _
6.      _ _ _ _ _ |_|_ _ _
```

A mystery word will appear inside the box. Write it here: _______________

UNIT 2 – THE COMMUNITY – LESSON 2 – WHERE'S THE MALL?
STUDENT BOOK PAGE 33

A. Prayer for Students & Self

B. Lesson Objective and Functions:
   - Asking for & describing location of places in the community

C. Grammar Structures:
   - Prepositions of Location

D. Biblical Reference or Principles:
   - John 14:4-6

E. Materials & Preparation:
   - For the Let's Practice Activity 3. Follow the Directions, create locations and street names on 8 ½ x 11 papers which appear on the map in the text. See more information under C. Conduct the Let's Practice Activity 3. Follow the Directions.

<u>Introduction</u>

Ask: "How do you get to ESL class? What streets do you go on?" Get student responses.

Say: "Today we are going to learn how to give directions."

Point out the vocabulary box, but don't teach it from this page.

UNIT 2
THE COMMUNITY

LESSON 2 – WHERE'S THE MALL?

Above: mall

Left: on the corner

<u>Places in the Community</u>

church

drug store

hospital

mall

post office

school

supermarket

<u>Prepositions of Location</u>

across from

next to

on the corner of

on the left

on the right

<u>Compass Directions</u>

east

north

south

west

UNIT 2 – THE COMMUNITY – LESSON 2 – WHERE'S THE MALL?
STUDENT BOOK PAGE 34

Introduce New Vocabulary

1. Have students open to Unit 2 – The Community; Lesson 2 – Where's the Mall?
2. Introduce the words or phrases with a repetition drill. For instruction on conducting repetition drills, see Activity Bank. Repeat each 5-6 times.
3. Elicit conversation about the places with questions, such as:

- Which churches are near to your house?
- Which drug store do you shop at?
- How close to the hospital is your house?
- Which supermarket do you shop at? Why?

church

drug store

hospital

supermarket

UNIT 2 – THE COMMUNITY – LESSON 2 – WHERE'S THE MALL?
STUDENT BOOK PAGE 35

1. Introduce the post office and church.
2. Demonstrate how a location can be on either the left or right depending on which way the speaker is facing.
3. Point out that Gumby's right hand is always pointing straight out while his left hand is always pointing up. Depending on which way he is facing (look for the eyes), the statement about the location of the post office and church will change.
4. Demonstrate in the classroom:
5. Place several large objects around the room across from each other. For example, place a table and a chair across from each other. Stand between the chair and the table facing toward the students. Make statements about the location of the table and chair according to which one is on your right and which is on your left. Turn away from the students and make statements about the location of the table and chair. The statements should now be the opposite of the first statements.
6. Place other objects around the room. Have students stand between each set of objects and make statements, then turn around and make additional statements.
7. Alternately, use a Gumby (often available in dollar stores) or similar object, plus objects or 8 ½ x 11 papers with locations printed on each one.

The post office is on Gumby's **<u>left.</u>**

The church is on Gumby's **<u>right</u>**.

post office church

The post office is on Gumby's **<u>right</u>**.

The church is on Gumby's **<u>left.</u>**

post office church

Look closely at Gumby. See his face in the picture above? Look at Gumby in the top picture. His face is turned away and you see the back of his head.

UNIT 2 – THE COMMUNITY – LESSON 2 – WHERE'S THE MALL?
STUDENT BOOK PAGE 36

Introduce ACROSS FROM and ACROSS THE STREET FROM and NEXT TO using the pictures.

Continue using objects in the room to make additional statements.

The Post Office is across the street from the church.

The Post Office is across from the church.

Post office church

The church is next to the school.

church school

UNIT 2 – THE COMMUNITY – LESSON 2 – WHERE'S THE MALL?
STUDENT BOOK PAGE 37

Introduce the directions north, south, east, west using the compass. Note that when reading a map, north is always toward the top of the map while south will be toward the bottom, east to the right side and west to the left side.

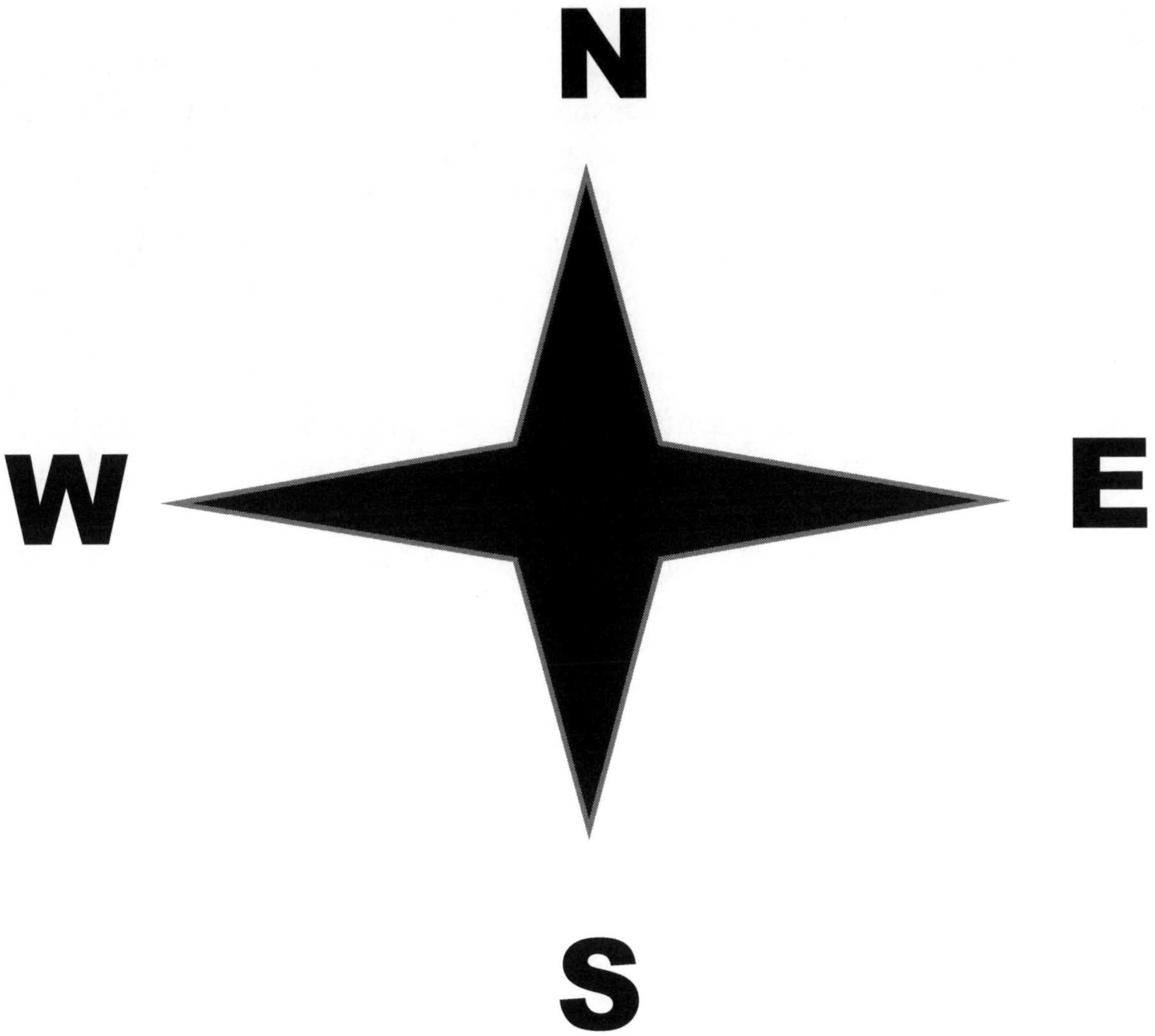

Compass		
	North	
West		East
	South	

UNIT 2 – THE COMMUNITY – LESSON 2 – WHERE'S THE MALL?
STUDENT BOOK PAGE 38

1. Have students turn books so East is to the right side.
2. Use the map to practice the compass directions north, south, east, west.
3. Pronounce the names of the streets on the map. Have students run their finger along the dotted line as the instructor names each street.
4. Name each location by its name and street located on.
5. Ask questions about the map, for example: "Where's the mall?" Encourage responses using the prepositions, for example: "The mall is on the corner of Pines Boulevard and Flamingo Road."
6. After all students have answered a question, begin a Chain Drill.
7. The instructor asks Student 1 a question, for example: "Where is the drug store?" Student 1 answers, "The drug store is on the corner of Pines Boulevard and Douglas Road."
8. Student 1 now asks a question of Student 2. Student 2 answers. Student 2 now asks a question of Student 3. Thus the Chain Drill is begun. Continue until the last student who asks his/her question of Student 1.

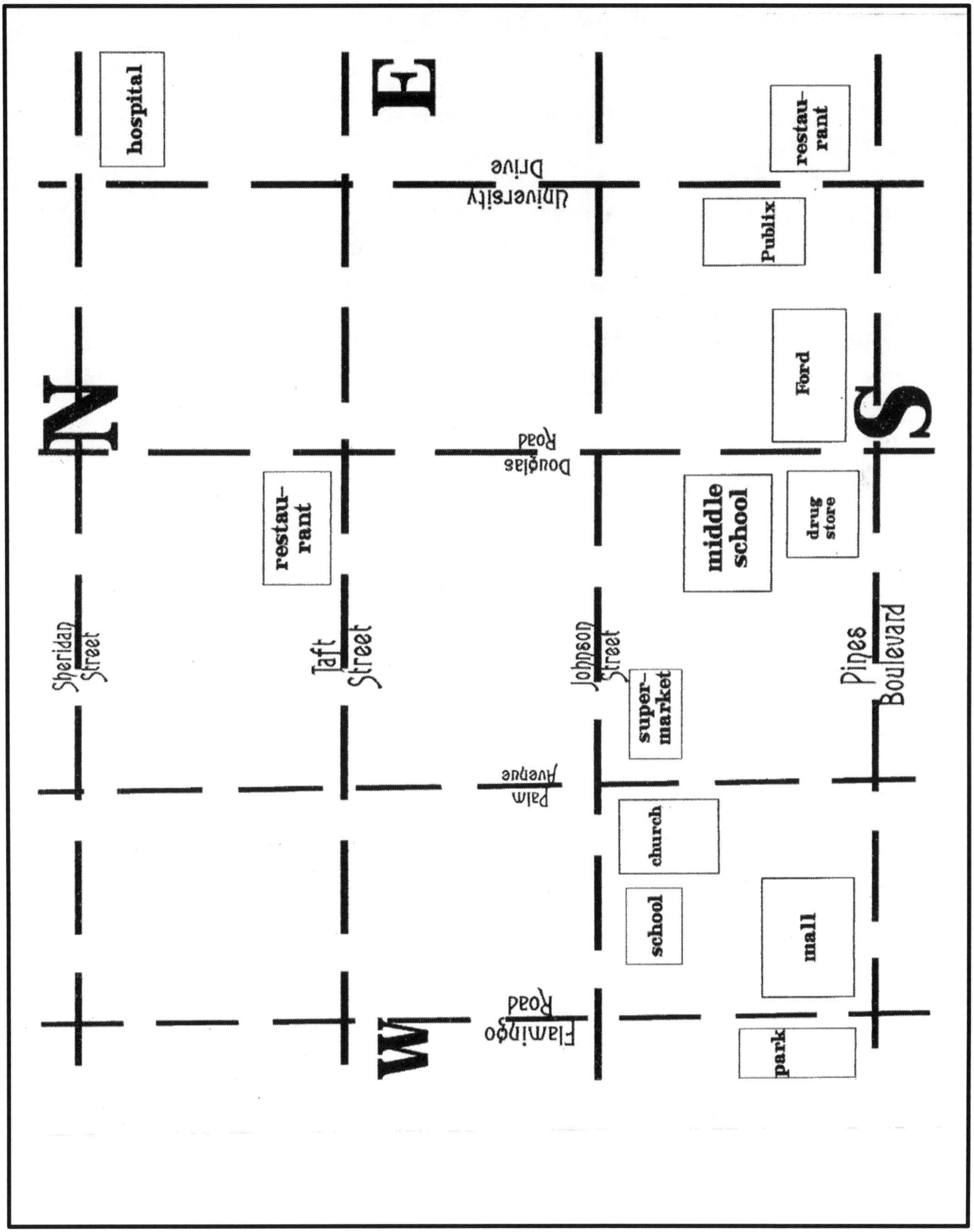
N
S
E
W
hospital
restaurant
restaurant
Publix
Ford
middle school
drug store
super-market
church
school
mall
park
University Drive
Douglas Road
Palm Avenue
Flamingo Road
Sheridan Street
Taft Street
Johnson Street
Pines Boulevard

UNIT 2 – THE COMMUNITY – LESSON 2 – WHERE'S THE MALL?
STUDENT BOOK PAGE 39

Time to Speak

A. Conversation Where's the Mall?

1. Ask: "Who are the 2 people in this conversation?"
2. Have students complete *To Do First* by having students repeat each line after the instructor. Repeat each line 5-6 times. Strive for a normal conversational tone rather than an oral reading tone.
3. Use backward build up for sentences longer than 4 words. Remember to divide sentences into sound units. See the Activity Bank for directions on backward build up and sound units.
4. Use correct intonation, stress, and rhythm patterns. Include the following intonation patterns:

- Statement (voice goes down at the end).
- WH-Question (voice starts high on the WH-Question word, drops in the middle of the sentence, then goes up and down on the last word.)

B. Have students complete *To Do Second* and *To Do Third*.
Call on individual student pairs to read the conversations after each Substitution has been drilled. Volunteer pairs present conversations for the class.

Time to Speak

Where's the Mall?

1.A. Where's the mall?

1.B. The **Pembroke Lakes Mall** is **on the corner of Pines Boulevard and Flamingo Road across from the Park.**

2.A. How do I get there from the school?

2.B. **Go west on Johnson Street to Flamingo Road. Turn south. The mall is on the left.**

3.A. Thanks.

Substitution No. 1

1.A. Excuse me. Where's the **church**?

1.B. **Pines Baptist Church is on the corner of Palm Avenue and Johnson Street next to the school.**

2.A. How do I get there from the school?

2.B. **Go east on Johnson Street to Palm Avenue. The church is on the right.**

3.A. Thanks.

Substitution Number 2

1.A. Excuse me. Where's the **drug store**?

1.B. **Walgreens Drug Store is on the corner of Douglas Road and Pines Boulevard.**

2.A. How do I get there from the school?

2.B. **Go east on Johnson Street to Douglas Road. Go south to Pines Boulevard. Walgreens is on the right.**

3.A. Thanks.

To Do First: Repeat the conversation after the instructor.

To Do Second: Speak with a partner. Change the underlined words for the Substitutions.

To Do Third: Change partners and repeat.

UNIT 2 – THE COMMUNITY – LESSON 2 – WHERE'S THE MALL?
STUDENT BOOK PAGE 40

Conclude Substitution Nos. 3 and 4.

Grammar Foundation

1. Complete *To Do First* by having students read the information under Prepositions of Location.
2. Have students complete *To Do Second* by having students repeat each example sentence after the instructor.
3. Ask for example sentences using the structures.

Substitution No. 3

1.A. Excuse me. Where's the **hospital**?

1.B. **Memorial Hospital Pembroke Pines is on the corner of Sheridan Street and University Drive.**

2.A. How do I get there from school?

2.B. **Go east on Johnson Street to University Drive. Go north on University Drive. The hospital is on the right**.

3.A. Thanks.

Substitution No. 4

1.A. Excuse me. Where's the **supermarket**?

1.B. **Winn Dixie Supermarket is on the corner of Palm Avenue and Johnson Street across from the church.**

2.A. How do I get there from the school?

2.B. **Go east on Johnson Street to Palm Avenue. Winn Dixie is across the street.**

3.A. Thanks.

Grammar Foundation

Prepositions of Location

Prepositions of Location are used to show the relationship of two objects to each other. Some common Prepositions of Location are: in, at, under, above, on, next to, between, across from, on the corner of, on the left, and on the right.

To Do First: Read the information.

To Do Second: Repeat example sentences after the instructor.

Noun	+ Be	+ Preposition	+ Noun
The hospital	is	on	Sheridan Street.
The bank	is	next to	the post office.
The church	is	across from	the supermarket.
The sofa	is	in	the living room.
The book	is	on	the table.

UNIT 2 – THE COMMUNITY – LESSON 2 – WHERE'S THE MALL?
STUDENT BOOK PAGE 41

Conclude the example sentences.

Let's Practice

A. Conduct the Let's Practice Activity 1. Map Directions – Listening Comprehension

1. Have students turn to the map page. Locate the church on the corner of Palm Avenue and Johnson Street.
2. Instructor gives directions to a location without telling students what the location is. For example, instructor gives directions to the hospital: "From the church, go north on Palm Avenue to Sheridan Street. Turn east. Go 2 blocks to University Drive. What's on the corner of University Drive and Sheridan Street?"
3. If students follow the directions correctly, they should arrive at the hospital. Students answer, "hospital."
4. Continue giving directions each time starting from the church.

B. Conduct the Let's Practice Activity 2. True/False Dictation

Have students put a marker in the page of the map and then turn to the Let's Practice Activity 2. True/False Dictation.
Instructor makes statements about the map. Repeat each statement at least 3 times.
Students consult their maps to see if the statement is true or false.
Students write the statement under the True or False columns.
Go over student responses.
Include these statements:

1. The park is on Flamingo Road. **True**
2. The middle school is on Palm Avenue. **False**
3. There are two restaurants on the map. **True**
4. The hospital is on Douglas Road. **False**
5. The supermarket is across from the church. **True**

My money	is	in	my purse.
The park	is	on the left.	
The mall	is	on the right.	
The restaurant	is	on the corner of	Douglas Road and Taft Street.

Let's Practice

1. Map Directions – Listening Comprehension

1. Turn in your books to the map with the compass directions of north, south, east, and west.
2. Locate the church on the corner of Palm Avenue and Johnson Street.
3. The instructor will give students directions to a location. Follow the directions. Say the location where you finish.

2. True/False Dictation

1. The instructor will dictate some statements about the map.
2. If the statement is TRUE, write it under the TRUE column.
3. If the reason is NOT True, write it under the FALSE column.

True	False
The school is on Johnson Street.	
	The mall is on Taft Street
1.	
2.	

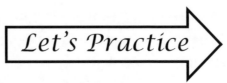

UNIT 2 – THE COMMUNITY – LESSON 2 – WHERE'S THE MALL?
STUDENT BOOK PAGE 42

C. Conduct the Let's Practice Activity 3. Follow the Directions

1. Instructor recreates the map from the book in the classroom.
2. Using 8 ½ x 11 papers, write one location from the map on each paper.
3. Create road signs using the street names from the map also on 8 ½ x 11 papers and affix them to chairs or desk tops to create street corners. Alternately, tape them to the floor to create intersections.
4. Along the floor, place the location papers on either side of the 'streets' which are defined by the placement of the 'street corner intersections.'
5. Instructor gives Student 1 directions to a location in the room, for example: "Walk north on University Drive, turn west on Taft Street. Go 1 block. Stop. Where are you?" Student 1 follows directions and should arrive to the restaurant.
6. Continue until all students have participated.

D. Conduct the Let's Practice Activity 4. Nelsigleny's New Neighborhood – Cloze Listening Activity **Teacher Answer Key and Transcript in Bold**

1. Instructor reads the paragraph. Students write the missing words on the lines.
2. Read at a normal speed. Assure students you will read as many times as students request.
3. When finished, go over student responses.

Nelsigleny's New Neighborhood

Nelsigleny just moved to a new neighborhood. She is learning her way around. Here's what she's found already. The **post office** is located on Taft Street. It's **across from** the restaurant. There's another **restaurant** on University Drive. She has her choice of two **supermarkets**. One **supermarket** is on the **corner of** Johnson Street and Palm Avenue and the other **supermarket** is on **University** Drive.

She works on the **corner of** University Drive and Sheridan Street. She's a dentist at the **hospital**. She loves to go shopping so she's real lucky that the **mall** is close by on the corner of Flamingo **Road** and **Pines** Boulevard. Nelsigleny is very happy with her new neighborhood.

3. ____

____

4. ____

____

5. ____

____

3. Follow the Directions

1. The instructor will recreate the map from the book in the classroom.
2. The instructor will give directions to a location. Student 1 follows the instructor's directions and arrives at a location.

4. Nelsigleny's New Neighborhood – Cloze Listening Activity

Listen to the instructor read the paragraph. Write the missing words on the lines.

Nelsigleny's New Neighborhood

Nelsigleny just moved to a new neighborhood. She is learning her way around. Here's what she's found already. The ***post office*** __________ is located on Taft Street. It's __________________ the restaurant. There's another __________________ on University Drive. She has her choice of two ______________. One ______________ is on the ______________ Johnson Street and Palm Avenue and the other ____________ ______________ is on ________________________ Drive.

She works on the ____________________University Drive and Sheridan Street. She's a dentist at the __________________. She loves to go shopping so she's real lucky that the ______________ is close by on the corner of Flamingo __________ and ___________ Boulevard. Nelsigleny is very happy with her new neighborhood.

UNIT 2 – THE COMMUNITY – LESSON 2 – WHERE'S THE MALL?
STUDENT BOOK PAGE 43

E. Conduct the Let's Practice Activity 5. Caret Listening Activity – John 14:4-6

1. Instructor reads the story at a normal speed. Assure students you will read as many times as they request.
2. Students listen for missing words.
3. Students put a slash [/] where they hear a word is missing. Students do not write the missing word; only put the slash mark. There are 10 missing words.
4. Demonstrate by reading the first line. Point out the slash mark already on student's paper as an example.
5. After the first reading, have students count the number of missing words they heard.
6. Then tell them there are 10 missing words. Students will probably then request instructor to read the passage again.
7. Missing words are in **bold.**
8. NOTE: This is the Biblical principle. When finished, instructor may wish to comment on the passage.

In the Bible Jesus **was** talking to his disciples one day. Jesus told **them** he was going away. The disciples didn't know **where** Jesus was going. Jesus was talking about going **to** Heaven. Here's what Jesus said to **his** disciples:
"You know the way to **the** place where I am going. Thomas said to him, "Lord, we don't know where **you** are going, so how can we know **the** way?" Jesus answered, "I am the way **and** the truth and the life. No one comes to **the** Father except through me." John 14:4-6

Review Exercises

Assign the Review Exercises for homework. Go over the instructions to ensure students understand how to complete each activity.
Answer Key in Bold

5. Caret Listening Activity – John 14:4-6

1. Listen to the teacher read the story.
2. When you hear that a word is missing, put a slash [/] where the word should be. See the example in the first line. Listen to the instructor read the first line.
3. Do not write the word.

In the Bible Jesus **/** talking to his disciples one day. Jesus told he was going away. The disciples didn't know Jesus was going. Jesus was talking about going Heaven. Here's what Jesus said to disciples:

"You know the way to place where I am going. Thomas said to him, "Lord, we don't know where are going, so how can we know way?" Jesus answered, "I am the way the truth and the life. No one comes to Father except through me." John 14:4-6.

Review Exercises

1. Write Directions

Write directions to two locations in YOUR neighborhood. Use the Prepositions of Location. Here's an example from the map in the book:

To go to the church from my house: 1. go west on Johnson Street to Palm Avenue. 2. Go south on Palm Avenue one block. 3. Go west on the first street. 4. Church is on the right.

____

____

____

____

____

____

____

____

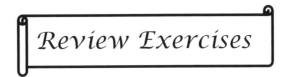

UNIT 2 – THE COMMUNITY – LESSON 2 – WHERE'S THE MALL?
STUDENT BOOK PAGE 44

2. Hidden Word Puzzle

Circle the words in the puzzle.

POST OFFICE	MALL	DRUG STORE	SUPERMARKET
HOSPITAL	NEXT TO	ACROSS FROM	ON THE CORNER

N K H K E W O J E S A T U S N K L Q I U W E O P Y U B V C X P U

A S D F G H K L N M B S D F G S A P Q I D N I U Y T R E W Q K K

L K J H H G F D S S A W N **P O S T O F F I C E** T O N M B V C X D

E N I O N W T Q J T H E M N I O P W N J N K L N I N E T N E L N

D G N X T C **O N T H E C O R N E R** X T T R M N N I O P Y T N B G

F M I V Y F A G E W Q U Y T R N B J A S M J F A T U N H E R N K

O Q **H O S P I T A L** W N K T N A N K E W Q O U B R N I Q W N E I

B T E W Q I Y W I C X S I N Q W E R R B N V C Q **M A L L** N I Y T

R E Q N I O N W T A L O H W A N Y S N I Y I O W T N Q I O U Y T

H N K A T N N I U Y E N M **S U P E R M A R K E T** L W O N T E W Q

N V J A L N Q W E R T Y I O P N K H G E N H H A Z I S W T I Y N

I W T R W O R K N N T N N I I O Y Y I I N I E T G D A B N I N E

N B X O N Q W E R T F R **N E X T T O** D E W B N I N O I N O T E N

I W O T O A S V T N I N K H I Y E N S T T H I M E S Q W E R T Y

U I O B M T **A C R O S S F R O M** T T N I N D A L S Y N I Y R T W

Q N M B X B V W T N I S E T D W **D R U G S T O R E** T I Y O W E N

A I Y I O P T A N D D I X X V B C N I Q T Y G A I X S S G T O T

2. Hidden Word Puzzle

Circle the words in the puzzle.

POST OFFICE MALL DRUG STORE SUPERMARKET

HOSPITAL NEXT TO ACROSS FROM ON THE CORNER

N K H K E W O J E S A T U S N K L Q I U W E O P Y U B V C X P U
A S D F G H K L N M B S D F G S A P Q I D N I U Y T R E W Q K K
L K J H H G F D S S A W N P O S T O F F I C E T O N M B V C X D
E N I O N W T Q J T H E M N I O P W N J N K L N I N E T N E L N
D G N X T C O N T H E C O R N E R X T T R M N N I O P Y T N B G
F M I V Y F A G E W Q U Y T R N B J A S M J F A T U N H E R N K
O Q H O S P I T A L W N K T N A N K E W Q O U B R N I Q W N E I
B T E W Q I Y W I C X S I N Q W E R R B N V C Q M A L L N I Y T
R E Q N I O N W T A L O H W A N Y S N I Y I O W T N Q I O U Y T
H N K A T N N I U Y E N M S U P E R M A R K E T L W O N T E W Q
N V J A L N Q W E R T Y I O P N K H G E N H H A Z I S W T I Y N
I W T R W O R K N N T N N I I O Y Y I I N I E T G D A B N I N E
N B X O N Q W E R T F R N E X T T O D E W B N I N O I N O T E N
I W O T O A S V T N I N K H I Y E N S T T H I M E S Q W E R T Y
U I O B M T A C R O S S F R O M T T N I N D A L S Y N I Y R T W
Q N M B X B V W T N I S E T D W D R U G S T O R E T I Y O W E N
A I Y I O P T A N D D I X X V B C N I Q T Y G A I X S S G T O T

UNIT 3 – LET'S EAT – LESSON 1 – AT THE DELI
STUDENT BOOK PAGE 45

A. Prayer for Students & Self

B. Lesson Objective and Functions:
- Ordering at a Deli

C. Grammar Structures:
- Using WOULD LIKE

D. Biblical Reference or Principles:
- John 6:35: Jesus said, / "I am the / bread of life. / He who / comes to me / will never go / hungry, and he / who believes in me / will never be / thirsty."

Introduction

1. Have students look at pictures of foods that can be found at a supermarket Deli counter. Point out which foods you like to eat.
2. After pointing out several foods, ask them to recall which foods you like to eat.
3. Ask students to point out which foods in the pictures they like to eat. Try to get responses from all students.
4. Say: "Today we are going to learn how to order foods at the Deli counter in the supermarket."
5. Point out the vocabulary box, but don't teach it from this page.

UNIT 3
LET'S EAT

LESSON 1 – AT THE DELI

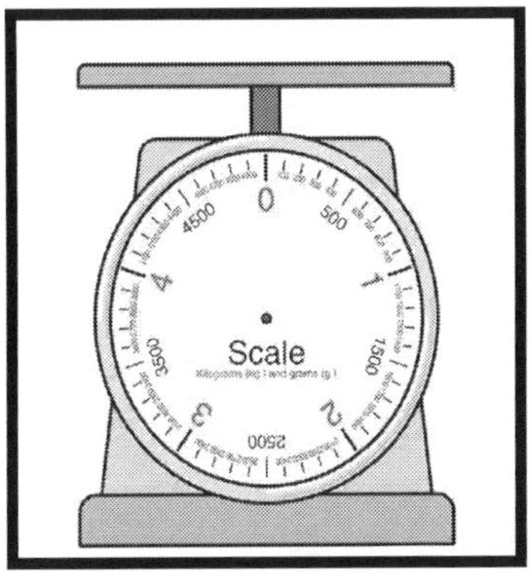

Measurements	Deli Products	Thickness
a quarter pound	cheddar cheese	very thin
a half pound	ham	thin
three quarters of a pound	provolone	medium
	roast beef	thick
a pound	Swiss cheese	very thick
	turkey	

UNIT 3 – LET'S EAT – LESSON 1 – AT THE DELI
STUDENT BOOK PAGE 46

Introduce New Vocabulary

1. Have students open to Unit 3 – Let's Eat; Lesson 1 – At the Deli.
2. Introduce the words or phrases with a repetition drill. For instruction on conducting repetition drills, see Activity Bank. Repeat each 5-6 times.
3. Elicit conversation about the various deli products by asking questions, such as:

- "Do you eat/like/dislike _________?"
- "Do you like to order at the Deli or buy prepackaged lunch meats and cheeses? Why?"

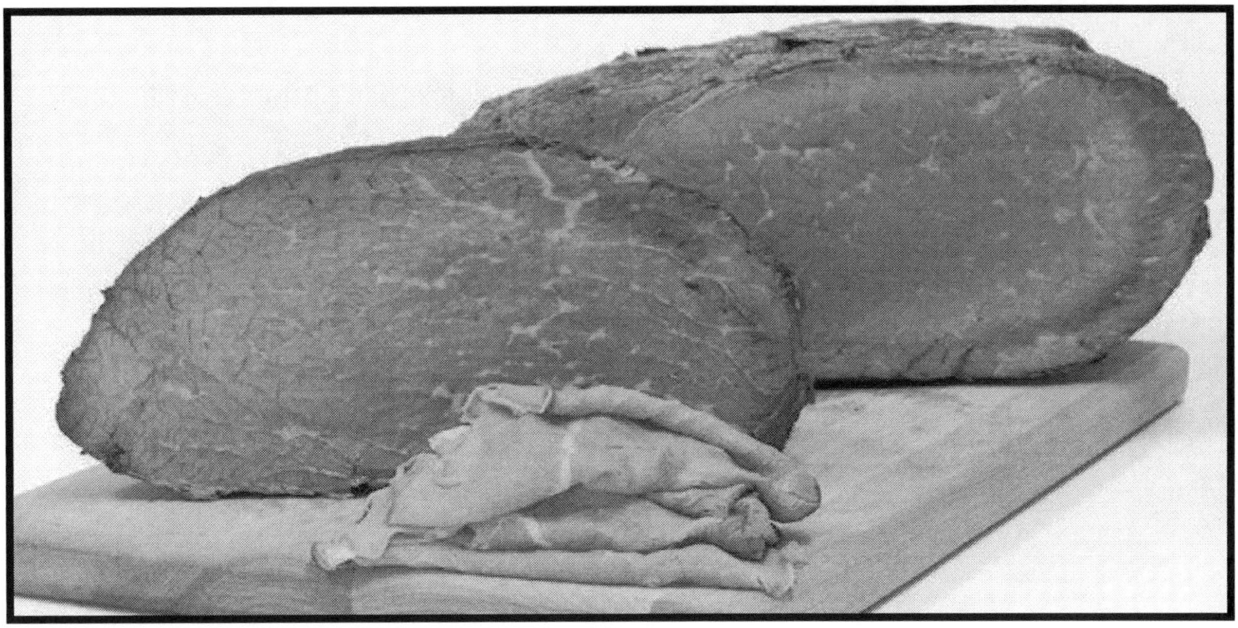

A pound of roast beef sliced very thin

Three quarters of a pound of ham sliced
sliced thin

A half pound of cheddar cheese
sliced very thick

UNIT 3 – LET'S EAT – LESSON 1 – AT THE DELI
STUDENT BOOK PAGE 47

1. Continue introducing the Deli products and the thickness options for slicing with repetition drill.

2. Discuss the pound system of measurement as opposed to the metric system. Compare the two systems. For equivalent amounts and a conversion chart, check out the Internet.

3. Note that a quarter pound is about equivalent to 100 grams.

4. Continue to elicit conversation by asking related questions.

A pound of provolone cheese sliced medium

A half pound of Swiss cheese sliced very thin

A quarter pound of turkey sliced very thin

UNIT 3 – LET'S EAT – LESSON 1 – AT THE DELI
STUDENT BOOK PAGE 48

Time to Speak

A. Conversation I'd Like a Quarter Pound of Turkey Breast.
   1. Ask: "Who are the 2 people in this conversation?"
   2. Have students complete *To Do First* by having students repeat each line after the instructor. Repeat each line 5-6 times. Strive for a normal conversational tone rather than an oral reading tone.
   3. Use backward build up for sentences longer than 4 words. Remember to divide sentences into sound units. See the Activity Bank for directions on backward build up and sound units.
   4. Use correct intonation, stress, and rhythm patterns. Include the following intonation patterns:
   - Statement (voice goes down at the end)
   - WH-Question (voice starts up, lowers in the middle of the sentence, then goes up and down on the last word)
   - YES/NO Question (voice goes up at the end), for example, "Anything else?"

B. Have students complete *To Do Second* and *To Do Third*.
Call on individual student pairs to read the conversations after each Substitution has been drilled. Volunteer pairs present conversations for the class.

Time to Speak

I'd Like a Quarter Pound of Turkey Breast

1.A. Now serving **number 21**.

1.B. Right here. I'd like **a quarter pound of turkey breast** **sliced thin**.

2.A. Here you are. Would you like anything else?

2.B. Yes. I'd like **a half pound of Swiss cheese** **sliced very thin**.

3.A. Here you are. Anything else?

3.B. No, that's all. Thank you.

To Do First: Repeat the conversation after the instructor.

To Do Second: Speak with a partner. Change the underlined words in the conversation for the Substitutions.

To Do Third: Change partners and repeat the Substitutions.

To Do Fourth: Change partners. What do you like to order?

Substitution No. 1

1.A. Now serving **number 22**.

1.B. Right here. I'd like **a pound of roast beef sliced very thin**.

2.A. Here you are. Would you like anything else?

2.B. Yes. I'd like **a pound of provolone cheese sliced medium**.

3.A. Here you are. Anything else?

3.B. No, that's all. Thank you.

Substitution No. 2

1.A. Now serving **number 23.**

1.B. Right here. I'd like **three quarters of a pound of ham sliced thin**.

2.A. Here you are. Would you like anything else?

2.B. Yes. I'd like **a half pound of cheddar cheese sliced very thick**.

3.A. Here you are. Anything else?

3.B. No, that's all. Thank you.

UNIT 3 – LET'S EAT – LESSON 1 – AT THE DELI
STUDENT BOOK PAGE 49

Grammar Foundation

1. Complete *To Do First* by having students read the information under Using WOULD LIKE to Express Preferences.
2. Have students complete *To Do Second* by having students repeat each example sentence after the instructor.
3. Ask for example sentences using the structures. Encourage use of the vocabulary words introduced.

Grammar Foundation

Using WOULD LIKE to Express Preferences

Use WOULD LIKE to express a preference or a choice of some action we want to do in the present or future or some thing we want to have in the present or future.

Affirmative

Subject +	WOULD LIKE +	Object or Infinitive Verb	Meaning of Sentence
I	would like	an apple.	I want an apple now.
You	would like	this book.	You want to read this book.
He	would like	a pound of cheese.	He wants a pound of cheese.
She	would like	some coffee.	She wants to drink some coffee now.
We	would like	to study English.	We want to study English.
They	would like	to go to the zoo.	They want to go to the zoo.

To Do First: Read the information about the grammar structure.

To Do Second: Repeat example sentences.

Negative

Subject +	WOULD + Not +	LIKE +	Object or Infinitive Verb
I	wouldn't	like	a half pound of Swiss cheese.
You	wouldn't	like	roast beef sliced very thin.
She	wouldn't	like	turkey breast sliced thick.
We	wouldn't	like	to shop at the deli.
They	wouldn't	like	ham sliced thin.

Questions

Question +	WOULD +	Subject +	LIKE +	Object or Infinitive	Answers
	Would	you	like	the ham sliced thin?	Yes, I would.
	Would	she	like	the cheese sliced thick?	No, she wouldn't.

UNIT 3 – LET'S EAT – LESSON 1 – AT THE DELI
STUDENT BOOK PAGE 50

Practicing Perfect Pronunciation

1. Introduce the /TH/ sound and demonstrate how to form the sound by placing the tip of the tongue slightly between the teeth and retracting it quickly as the word is formed.
2. Ensure students that it is NOT rude behavior to show the tongue in order the form the /TH/ sound. In fact, the sound cannot be formed without placing the tongue between the teeth. The tendency is to place the tongue tip behind the front teeth, but the resulting sound is a /d/, /t/, or even an /s/.
3. Practice the words with /TH/ from the conversation.
4. Drill the lines of the tongue twister Thick 'n Thin with a repetition drill. Be sure to say it quickly. Also remember the intonation patterns of AND/OR (voice goes up on first choice, down on the AND or OR, and then up and down on the second choice), WH-Question (voice starts high on the WH-Question word, drops in the middle of the sentence, then goes up and then down on the last word), and the Statement intonation pattern (voice goes down at the end).
5. Call on volunteer pairs to present Thick 'n Thin to the class.

Let's Practice

A. Conduct the Let's Practice Activity 1. Who Says It? Dictation

1. Instructor dictates statements taken from the conversation and substitutions, see below. Repeat each statement 3 times.
2. Students write the statement under the columns Customer Says and Deli Employee Says.
3. Go over student responses.

Include these statements:

Customer Says	Deli Employee Says
1.	***Now serving number 3.***

	Would	he	like	the provolone sliced?	No, he wouldn't.
	Would	they	like	some coffee?	Yes, they would.
What	would	you	like	on your sandwich?	I'd like ham and cheese.
When	wouldyour mother like			to come to Florida?	She'd like to come in May.
Where	would	they	like	the sofa?	In the living room.
Why	would	they	like	to go to the beach?	Because they like to swim.

~~*Practicing Perfect Pronunciation*~~

1. Form the /TH/ by placing the tip of the tongue slightly between the teeth and retracting it quickly as the word is formed.
2. Practice the /TH/ sound with these words from the conversation:

   thick thin very thin thank you three quarters of a pound
3. Repeat this conversation after the instructor.

<u>Thick 'n Thin</u>

By Barbara K. Black

1.A. I would like three quarters of a pound.

1.B. How would you like it sliced? Thick or thin?

2.A. Let me think. Thick or thin? Thick or thin? Thick or thin? How about very thin.

2.B. O.K. Here's three quarters of a pound sliced thin.

3.A. I thought I said very thin?

3.B. Thick or thin? Thick or thin? Thick or thin? Oh, yes, you said very thin.

4.A. Yes, very thin.

4.B. Here you are, then. Thank you and come again!

UNIT 3 – LET'S EAT – LESSON 1 – AT THE DELI
STUDENT BOOK PAGE 51

2. **I'd like a half pound of Swiss cheese.**
3. **Would you like anything else?**
4. **Here you are.**
5. **No, that's all.**

B. Conduct the Let's Practice Activity 2. Listening to Deli Orders

1. Instructor reads the conversation using two different voices for A & B. Read each conversation all the way through 3 times.
2. To help students keep their place, say, "1.A. and 1.B." before each line.
3. Alternately, if a second instructor is available, use two instructors.

Conversation A.

1.A. Now serving **number 8**.

1.B. Right here. I'd like **a half** pound of **ham** sliced **very thin**.

2.A. Here you are. Would you like anything else?

2.B. Yes. I'd like **a quarter** pound of **cheddar cheese** sliced **thin**.

3.A. Would you like anything else today?

3.B. No, that's all. Thank you.

4.A. You're welcome. Have a nice day.

4.B. You too.

Conversation B.

1.A. Now serving **number 32**.

1.B. Right here. I'd like **three quarters of a** pound of **Swiss cheese** sliced **thick**.

2.A. Here you are. Would you like anything else?

2.B. Yes. I'd like **a quarter** pound of **roast beef** sliced **medium**.

3.A. Would you like anything else today?

3.B. No, that's all. Thank you.

4.A. You're welcome. Have a nice day.

4.B. You too.

Let's Practice

1. Who Says It? Dictation

The instructor will dictate some statements. If the statement is one that a customer says, write it under the Customer column. If the statement is one that a Deli employee says, write it under the Deli Employee column.

Customer Says	Deli Employee Says
1.	***Now serving number 3.***
2.	
3.	
4.	
5.	

2. Listening to Deli Orders

Conversation A.

1.A. Now serving ______________________.

1.B. Right here. I'd like__________________pound of ____________sliced ______________________.

2.A. Here you are. Would you like anything else?

2.B. Yes. I'd like _________________pound of __________________ sliced ________________.

3.A. Would you like anything else today?

3.B. No, that's all. Thank you.

4.A. You're welcome. Have a nice day.

4.B. You too.

Conversation B.

1.A. Now serving _________________.

1.B. Right here. I'd like __________________________ pound of __________ sliced ________________.

2.A. Here you are. Would you like anything else?

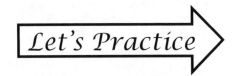

UNIT 3 – LET'S EAT – LESSON 1 – AT THE DELI
STUDENT BOOK PAGE 52

Conversation C.

1.A. Now serving **number 25** .

1.B. Right here. I'd like **a** pound of **provolone cheese** sliced **very thin**.

2.A. Here you are. Would you like anything else?

2.B. Yes. I'd like **a half** pound of **smoked turkey** sliced **very thick** .

3.A. Would you like anything else today?

3.B. No, that's all. Thank you.

4.A. You're welcome. Have a nice day.

4.B. You too.

C. Conduct the Let's Practice Activity 3. Scrambled Sentence

1. Work with a partner to put the sentence into correct order.
2. Read your completed sentence to the class.
3. This is the Biblical principle. When finished, instructor may wish to comment on the verse.

NOTE: The divisions shown are those in student text.

John 6:35: Jesus said, / "I am the / bread of life. / He who / comes to me / will never go / hungry, and he / who believes in me / will never be / thirsty."

2.B. Yes. I'd like ________________pound of_____________ sliced___________.

3.A. Would you like anything else today?

3.B. No, that's all. Thank you.

4.A. You're welcome. Have a nice day.

4.B. You too.

Conversation C.

1.A. Now serving ______________________.

1.B. Right here. I'd like _____pound of __________________ sliced __________.

2.A. Here you are. Would you like anything else?

2.B. Yes. I'd like ___________pound of__________________ sliced___________.

3.A. Would you like anything else today?

3.B. No, that's all. Thank you.

4.A. You're welcome. Have a nice day.

4.B. You too.

3. Scrambled Sentence

1. Work with a partner to put the sentence into correct order.
2. Write the completed sentence on the line.
3. Read your completed sentence to the class.

UNIT 3 – LET'S EAT – LESSON 1 – AT THE DELI
STUDENT BOOK PAGE 53

D. Conduct the Let's Practice Activity 4. Pair, Square, Share

1. Pairs of students interview each other.
2. After both partners share, each pair then joins another pair to make a group of 4 (a square).
3. The original partners summarize their partner's responses to this group of 4. Continue until all students have summarized their original partner's responses.
4. If desired, ask for original partners to summarize their partner's responses for the class.

John 6:35: will never go / "I am the / He who / thirsty." / comes to me / who believes in me / hungry, and he / bread of life. / Jesus said, / will never be /

____

____

4. Pair, Square, Share

1. Work with a partner. Student 1 asks: "What foods do you like to order from the Deli?"
2. Student 2 answers.
3. Student 2 asks: "What foods do you like to order from the Deli?"
4. Student 1 answers.
5. When finished, listen for the instructor's instructions.

UNIT 3 – LET'S EAT – LESSON 1 – AT THE DELI
STUDENT BOOK PAGE 54

Review Exercises

Assign the Review Exercises for homework. Go over the instructions to ensure students understand how to complete each activity.

Answer Key in Bold

1. Hidden Word Puzzle

Circle the hidden words in the puzzle.

D L K J **R O A S T B E E F** K L U I O P E N M N B K L U Y

C H E D D A R C H E E S E L K H E N I O W E V D S G H S

T H R E E Q U A R T E R S O F A P O U N D K H K **H A M** K

L I Y T E Q E T K N M I Y N O P U E N F D S A A K N M K

O P L **T H I N** K N B N **T H I C K** H N T **V E R Y T H I N** K

H K L G F D **M E D I U M** E N W J K L N M B V C D W E R Q

A **P R O V O L O N E** W J K L F E E W N I O P N W B S D F

W Q J M N **Q U A R T E R P O U N D** I Q A S D F G B V C O

E S L W U E G S L D D S A **C H E D D A R C H E E S E** E B

P O U N D K N **S L I C E D** J N **H A L F P O U N D** I Y E W

Q A S D F G J K L U Y T E E M N B V C X E I O W W Q A S

G G Z Z A **S W I S S C H E E S E** T Y U I Z X C V B N F G

H J K Q W E R **T U R K E Y** I O P H J K N N J K L D F N B

B S A M B V **C U S T O M E R** N N **D E L I C O U N T E R** A

S E R V I N G N B C A S D F G **T I C K E T N U M B E R** N

K I A S N K N K L S D G G **S E R V I N G** Q E Y U I O E Q

A S D F G H J K L N K U N E T N K H **S L I C E D** N V C X

Review Exercises

1. Hidden Word Puzzle

Circle the hidden words in the puzzle.

D L K J R O A S T B E E F K L U I O P E N M N B K L U Y
C H E D D A R C H E E S E L K H E N I O W E V D S G H S
T H R E E Q U A R T E R S O F A P O U N D K H K H A M K
L I Y T E Q E T K N M I Y N O P U E N F D S A A K N M K
O P L T H I N K N B N T H I C K H N T V E R Y T H I N K
H K L G F D M E D I U M E N W J K L N M B V C D W E R Q
A P R O V O L O N E W J K L F E E W N I O P N W B S D F
W Q J M N Q U A R T E R P O U N D I Q A S D F G B V C O
E S L W U E G S L D D S A C H E D D A R C H E E S E E B
P O U N D K N S L I C E D J N H A L F P O U N D I Y E W
Q A S D F G J K L U Y T E E M N B V C X E I O W W Q A S
G G Z Z A S W I S S C H E E S E T Y U I Z X C V B N F G
H J K Q W E R T U R K E Y I O P H J K N N J K L D F N B
B S A M B V C U S T O M E R N N D E L I C O U N T E R A
S E R V I N G N B C A S D F G T I C K E T N U M B E R N
K I A S N K N K L S D G G S E R V I N G Q E Y U I O E Q
A S D F G H J K L N K U N E T N K H S L I C E D N V C X

UNIT 3 – LET'S EAT – LESSON 1 – AT THE DELI
STUDENT BOOK PAGE 55

2. Correct the Mistakes

1. Each sentence has some mistakes.
2. Correct the mistakes.
3. Write the correct sentence on the line.

1. Would you to order now? ***Would you like to order now?***
2. Would you like any else? **Would you like anything else?**
3. Here you is. **Here you are.**
4. I like a pound of roast beef sliced very thin. **I would like a pound of roast beef sliced very thin.**
5. Please slice the cheese tick. **Please slice the cheese thick.**
6. Now serving number B. **Now serving number (any number; not letter).**
7. He would some roast beef and some turk. **He would like some roast beef and some turkey.**

2. Correct the Mistakes

1. Each sentence has some mistakes.
2. Correct the mistakes.
3. Write the correct sentence on the line.

1. Would you to order now? ***Would you like to order now?***

2. Would you like any else? ______

3. Here you is. ______

4. I like a pound of roast beef sliced very thin. ______

______

5. Please slice the cheese tick. ______

6. Now serving number B. ______

7. He would some roast beef and some turk. ______

______

UNIT 3 – Let's Eat – Lesson 2 – The Six Food Groups
STUDENT BOOK PAGE 56

A. Prayer for Students & Self

B. Lesson Objective and Functions:
   - Identifying foods in each of the six food groups

C. Grammar Structures:
   - Using SOME and ANY

D. Biblical Reference or Principles:
   - Various Scriptures about food including: Genesis 2:16; 9:3-4; Proverbs 26:16; 23:20-21.

E. Materials & Preparation:
   - For the Let's Practice Activity 3. Food Groups Ball Toss – a koosh ball. Alternately, use a wadded up piece of paper or other soft object to toss.

<u>Introduction</u>

1. Look at the picture of the Six Food Groups. Identify the foods in the picture.
2. Ask: "Which of these foods do you like to eat? Which of these foods do you NOT like to eat?"
3. Ask: "Have you heard about the six food groups before? What do you know about the six food groups?"
4. Say: "Today we are going to learn about the six food groups and what kinds of foods go into each group. It is important to eat from all six groups every day to be healthy."

UNIT 3
LET'S EAT

LESSON 2 – THE SIX FOOD GROUPS

The Six Food Groups

Bread: whole grain bread, rice

Fruit: apples and bananas

Vegetable: lettuce and tomato

Meat: chicken and fish

Milk: yogurt and cheese

Fat: olive oil, butter and pecans

UNIT 3 – Let's Eat – Lesson 2 – The Six Food Groups
STUDENT BOOK PAGE 57

Introduce New Vocabulary

1. Have students open to Unit 3 – Let's Eat; Lesson 2 – The Six Food Groups.
2. Introduce the words or phrases with a repetition drill. For instruction on conducting repetition drills, see Activity Bank. Repeat each 5-6 times.
3. Elicit conversation by asking questions about the pictures, for example:

- "What kinds of foods do you see in the bread/vegetable/fruit/meat food group?'
- "What other types of vegetables/fruits/meats can you name?"

bread food group

vegetable food group

fruit food group

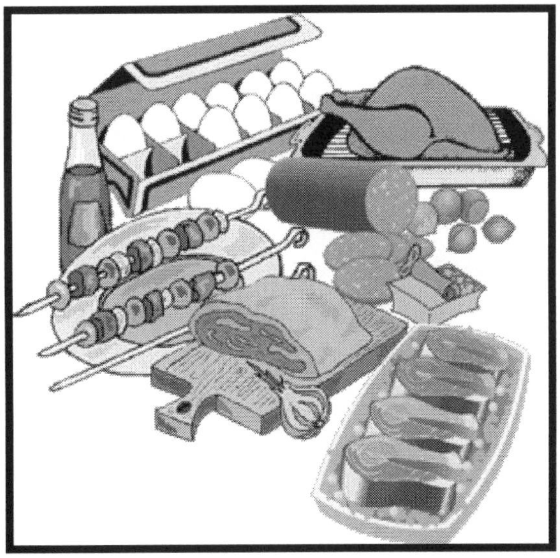

meat food group

UNIT 3 – Let's Eat – Lesson 2 – The Six Food Groups
STUDENT BOOK PAGE 58

Continue introducing the words and phrases with a repetition drill.
Continue eliciting conversation with questions.

milk food group

fat food group

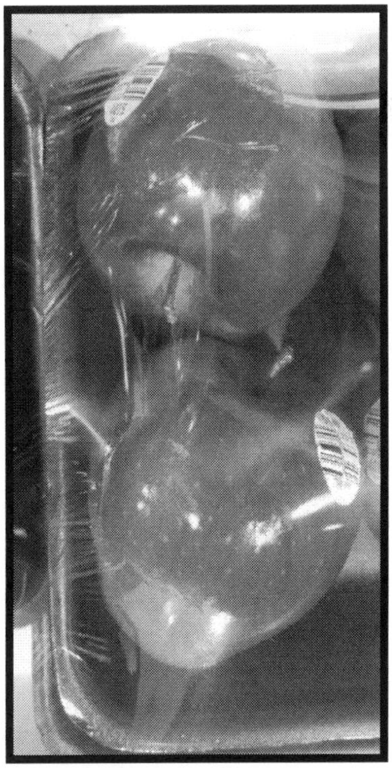

Above: rice

Right: apples

UNIT 3 – Let's Eat – Lesson 2 – The Six Food Groups
STUDENT BOOK PAGE 59

Continue introducing foods with repetition drill and
Eliciting conversation through questions.

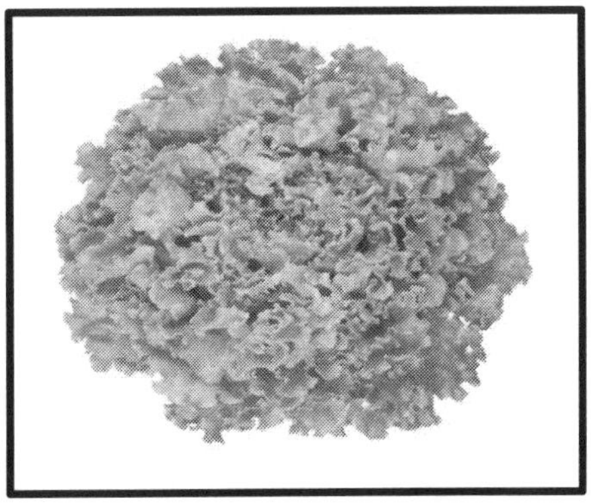

Top Left: yogurt

Top Right: chicken

Above Middle: pasta

Above Right: olive oil

Left: bananas

Above: lettuce

UNIT 3 – Let's Eat – Lesson 2 – The Six Food Groups
STUDENT BOOK PAGE 60

Continue introducing foods with repetition drill and
Eliciting conversation through questions.

Note that candy and ice cream would fit into the Fat food group, but it should be eaten only occasionally and not in place of olive oil and other good fats.

Barbara Kinney Black

Above: tomato

Above Right: fish

Above: cheese Right: butter

Far left:

candy

Left:

Ice cream

UNIT 3 – Let's Eat – Lesson 2 – The Six Food Groups
STUDENT BOOK PAGE 61

Time to Speak

A. Conversation The Six Food Groups

1. Ask: "Who are the 2 people in this conversation?"
2. Have students complete *To Do First* by having students repeat each line after the instructor. Repeat each line 5-6 times. Strive for a normal conversational tone rather than an oral reading tone.
3. Use backward build up for sentences longer than 4 words. Remember to divide sentences into sound units. See the Activity Bank for directions on backward build up and sound units.
4. Use correct intonation, stress, and rhythm patterns. Include the following intonation patterns:

- Statement (voice goes down at the end).
- Yes/No Question (voice goes up at the end).

B. Have students complete *To Do Second* and *To Do Third*.
Call on individual student pairs to read the conversations after each Substitution has been drilled. Volunteer pairs present conversations for the class.

Point out the vocabulary box, but don't teach it from this page.

Time to Speak

The Six Food Groups

1.A. **Marlene,** did you have foods from all six food groups today?

1.B. Yes, mother. From the Bread group I had some **rice**. From the Fruit group I had **an apple**. From the Vegetable group I had **some lettuce**. From the Meat group I had **some chicken**. From the Milk group I had **some yogurt**. From the Fat group I had **some butter** on my **rice**.

2.A. Did you have **any candy?**

2.B. No, I didn't.

To Do First: Repeat the conversation after the instructor.

To Do Second: Speak with a partner. Change the underlined words in the conversation for the Substitutions.

To Do Third: Change partners. Use the conversation to talk about yourselves.

Substitution No. 1

1.A. **Carlos**, did you have foods from all six food groups today?

1.B. Yes, mother. From the Bread group I had **some pasta**. From the Fruit group I had **a banana**. From the Vegetable group I had **a tomato**. From the Meat group I had **some fish**. From the Milk group I had **some cheese**. From the Fat group I had **some olive oil** on my **pasta**.

2.A. Did you have **any ice cream?**

2.B. No, I didn't.

Food Groups		Foods		Articles
bread	apple	fish	tomato	a
fat	banana	ice cream	yogurt	an
fruit	butter	lettuce		some
meat	candy	olive oil		any
milk	cheese	pasta		
vegetable	chicken	rice		

UNIT 3 – Let's Eat – Lesson 2 – The Six Food Groups
STUDENT BOOK PAGE 62

Grammar Foundation

1. Complete *To Do First* by having students read the information under Using A, AN, SOME, and ANY with Nouns.
2. Have students complete *To Do Second* by having students repeat each example sentence after the instructor.
3. Ask for example sentences using the structures.

Complete the Sentences. Use A, AN, SOME, and ANY. **Teacher Answer Key in Bold**

1. I had ***an*** apple for lunch.
2. John ate ***a*** banana yesterday.
3. She would like ***some*** rice.
4. Would you like **any/some** pasta?
5. Gladys ate **some** lettuce and **a** tomato for lunch.
6. "Romilio," Zelda asked. "Do we have **any** chicken in the refrigerator?"
7. "No," Romilio answered. "We don't have **any** more chicken."
8. I bought **some** rice, **some** olive oil, **an** apple, and **a** banana at the supermarket.
9. Carmen didn't eat **any** turkey or yogurt for lunch.
10. "Did you get **any** butter or **any** fish at the supermarket?" asked Bernie.
11. "I bought **some** butter, but I am going fishing tonight so will catch **some** fish then," Adel replied.

Grammar Foundation

Using A, AN, SOME, and ANY with Nouns

1. Use the Article 'A' in front of Singular Count Nouns. Count Nouns are those that can be counted, for example, bananas. We can count 1 banana, 2 bananas, 3 bananas, etc.
2. Use the Article 'AN' in front of Singular Count Nouns that begin with a vowel, for example: an apple, an egg, an orange, an ice cream cone, an umbrella, etc.
3. Use the Article 'SOME' in a Statement in front of Plural Count Nouns, for example: some apples, some tomatoes.
4. Use the Article 'SOME' in a Statement in front of Noncount Nouns. Noncount Nouns have no plural form and we cannot count individual pieces. For example: some rice, some cheese, some butter, some olive oil, some yogurt, some bread, some milk.
5. Use 'ANY' to make a Negative Statement for Plural Count Nouns and Noncount Nouns, for example: I don't have any tomatoes. (plural count noun) We didn't eat any fruit. (noncount noun) They don't have any chicken. (noncount noun) We don't have any apples. (plural count noun)
6. Use 'ANY' or 'SOME' in a Question, for example: Did you eat any lettuce? = Did you eat some lettuce?

To Do First: Read the information about the grammar structure.

To Do Second: Repeat the example sentences.

Complete the Sentences. Use A, AN, SOME, and ANY.

1. I had ***an***___ apple for lunch.
2. John ate __ ***a*** ___ banana yesterday.
3. She would like ___ ***some*** rice.
4. Would you like __ ***any/some*** __ pasta?
5. Gladys ate ___________ lettuce and ______tomato for lunch.
6. "Romilio," Zelda asked. "Do we have ___________ chicken in the refrigerator?"
7. "No," Romilio answered. "We don't have _______ more chicken."
8. I bought ________ rice, ___________ olive oil, ________ apple, and ______ banana at the supermarket.
9. Carmen didn't eat ___________ turkey or yogurt for lunch.
10. "Did you get __________ butter or _____________ fish at the supermarket?" asked Bernie.
11. "I bought _____________butter, but I am going fishing tonight so will catch ______ _____ fish then," Adel replied.

UNIT 3 – Let's Eat – Lesson 2 – The Six Food Groups
STUDENT BOOK PAGE 63

Practicing Perfect Pronunciation

Series of Items – The voice rises at the comma after each item in the list, lowers just before the final item at AND, then drops at the end of the final item as in Statement intonation.

For example, "In the Bread group we have rice, bread, and pasta." The voice rises at the commas after rice and bread, then drops for the word AND, then rises and drops on the final word, pasta.

Repeat the following after the instructor:

1. Pasta, pineapple, turkey, broccoli, yogurt, and butter.
2. Tomatoes, apples, and rice.
3. Fish, bananas, cheese, lettuce, yogurt, and chicken.
4. Galatians 5:22-23 says, "The fruit of the Spirit is love, joy, peace, patience, kindness, goodness, faithfulness, gentleness, and self-control."

Let's Practice

A. Conduct the Let's Practice Activity 1. Answer Questions about the Conversation

1. Have students look at the conversation "The Six Food Groups."
2. Instructor asks the question Nos. 3.-7. Repeat each question 3-4 times while students are searching for and writing the answers.
3. Students write their answers on the lines.
4. Go over student responses with the class.

1. Did Marlene have any rice? ***Yes, she did.***
2. Did Carlos have any yogurt? ***No, he didn't.***
3. Did Marlene have an apple? **Yes, she did.**

~~*Practicing Perfect Pronunciation*~~

Series of Items Intonation Pattern

In the Series of Items Intonation Pattern, the voice rises at the comma after each item in the list, lowers at AND just before the final item, then drops at the end of the final item as in Statement intonation.

For example, "In the Bread group we have rice, bread, and pasta." The voice raises at the commas after rice and bread, then drops for the word AND, then raises and drops on the final word, pasta.

Repeat the following after the instructor:

1. Pasta, pineapple, turkey, broccoli, yogurt, and butter
2. Tomatoes, apples, and rice.
3. Fish, bananas, cheese, lettuce, yogurt, and chicken
4. Galatians 5:22-23 says, "The fruit of the Spirit is love, joy, peace, patience, kindness, goodness, faithfulness, gentleness, and self-control."

Let's Practice

1. Answer Questions about the Conversation

1. Look at the conversation "The Six Food Groups."
2. The instructor will ask some questions. Write your answers on the lines.
3. Go over your responses with the class.

1. Did Marlene have any rice? ***Yes, she did.*** ____________________

2. Did Carlos have any yogurt? ***No, he didn't.*** ____________________

3. ____

UNIT 3 – Let's Eat – Lesson 2 – The Six Food Groups
STUDENT BOOK PAGE 64

4. Did Marlene have any ice cream? **No, she didn't.**
5. Did Carlos have any pasta with olive oil? **Yes, he did.**
6. Did Marlene have any candy? **No, she didn't.**
7. Did Carlos and Marlene eat from all six food groups? **Yes, they did.**

B. Conduct the Let's Practice Activity 2. The Add On Game

1. Student 1 makes a statement, for example: "I'm going to the store to buy some apples."
2. Student 2 repeats Student 1's statement and adds his/her own statement, for example, "I'm going to the store to buy some apples and bananas."
3. Continue repeating and adding food words with the next letter of the alphabet until all have participated. Encourage use of the new vocabulary and other known words.

C. Conduct the Let's Practice Activity 3. Food Groups Ball Toss

1. The instructor will say a food group, for example: vegetable group, and toss a koosh ball to Student 1.
2. Student 1 names a food in that group, for example: tomatoes, and tosses the ball back to the instructor.
3. Encourage the use of the vocabulary and other known food words.
4. Continue until all have participated multiple times.

D. Conduct the Let's Practice Activity 4. Survey

1. Students talk to their classmates and ask: "What foods did you eat in each food group yesterday?"
2. Students write their classmates' responses on their surveys under the correct food group column.
3. Volunteers share their classmates' responses with the class.

Name	Bread	Fruit	Vegetable	Meat	Milk	Fat
Barbara	***pasta***	***pineapple***	***broccoli***	***turkey***	***yogurt***	***butter***

4. ______________________________

5. ______________________________

6. ______________________________

7. ______________________________

2. Play the Add On Game

1. Student 1 makes a statement, for example: "I'm going to the store to buy some apples."
2. Student 2 repeats Student 1's statement and adds a food word beginning with the letter 'B', for example, "I'm going to the store to buy some apples and bananas."
3. Student 3 repeats Student 1 and 2's statements and adds a food word beginning with the letter 'C'.
4. Continue repeating and adding food words with the next letter of the alphabet until all have participated.

3. Food Groups Ball Toss

1. The instructor will say a food group, for example: vegetable group, and toss a ball to Student 1.
2. Student 1 names a food in that group, for example: tomatoes, and tosses the ball back to the instructor.

4. Survey

1. Talk to your classmates. Ask: "What foods did you eat in each food group yesterday?"
2. Write their responses on your survey under the correct food group column.

Name	Bread	Fruit	Vegetable	Meat	Milk	Fat
Barbara	*pasta*	*pineapple*	*broccoli*	*turkey*	*yogurt*	*butter*

UNIT 3 – Let's Eat – Lesson 2 – The Six Food Groups
STUDENT BOOK PAGE 65

E. Conduct the Let's Practice Activity 5. Listening Activity

1. Listen to the instructor read the passage. Circle the word [in brackets] that you hear.
2. Go over responses with the class.

NOTE: This is the Biblical principle. When finished, instructor may wish to comment on the passage. **Teacher Answer Key and Transcript in Bold.**

The Scripture says a lot about food. For example, in Genesis 2:16, "The Lord God [command / **commanded**] Adam, 'You may eat the [**fruit** / fat] from any tree in the garden. But you must not eat the fruit from the tree which gives the knowledge of [grapes / **good**] and evil. If you ever eat [fat / **fruit**] from that tree, you will die!'" Well, we know what happened after Eve ate the fruit! In Genesis 9:3 and 4, God tells Noah after the flood, "Earlier I gave you the [great / **green**] plants. And now I give you everything for [**food** / free], but you must not eat meat that still has blood in it." In Proverbs 25:16, we read, "If you find honey, don't eat too [many / **much**]. Too much of it will make you sick." Then in Proverbs 23:20-21, we read, "Don't be one of those who drink too much wine or who [ate / **eat**] too much food. Those who drink too much and eat too [many / **much**] become poor. They sleep too much and end up wearing rags." So, no matter what you eat, it's a good idea to eat some [food / **foods**] from all six food groups every day.

Review Exercises

Assign the Review Exercises for homework. Go over the instructions to ensure students understand how to complete each activity.
Answer Key in Bold

5. Listening Activity

1. Listen to the instructor read the passage. Circle the word [in brackets] that you hear.
2. Go over responses with the class.

The Scripture says a lot about food. For example, in Genesis 2:16, "The Lord God [command / commanded] Adam, 'You may eat the [fruit / fat] from any tree in the garden. But you must not eat the fruit from the tree which gives the knowledge of [grapes / good] and evil. If you ever eat [fat / fruit] from that tree, you will die!'" Well, we know what happened after Eve ate the fruit! In Genesis 9:3 and 4, God tells Noah after the flood, "Earlier I gave you the[great / green] plants. And now I give you everything for [food / free], but you must not eat meat that still has blood in it." In Proverbs 25:16, we read, "If you find honey, don't eat too [many / much]. Too much of it will make you sick." Then in Proverbs 23:20-21, we read, "Don't be one of those who drink too much wine or who [ate / eat] too much food. Those who drink too much and eat too [many / much] become poor. They sleep too much and end up wearing rags." So, no matter what you eat, it's a good idea to eat some [food / foods] from all six food groups every day.

Review Exercises

1. Complete the Sentences with your own Words

Use your own words to complete the sentences.

1. I'm going to the supermarket. I need to buy some ________________________ ____ and a ______________, and an __________________.
2. Ruth ate a ________________ and an __________________ for breakfast.
3. Do we have any _________________ or some _________________?
4. Would you like an ____________________ for lunch?
5. Tom didn't eat any ______________ for dinner last night.

UNIT 3 – Let's Eat – Lesson 2 – The Six Food Groups
STUDENT BOOK PAGE 66

2. Scrambled Sentence

Put the words of the sentences into correct order.

1. **Would you buy some rice and some pasta when you go to the supermarket?**
   when you go / to the supermarket / Would you buy / some pasta / some rice and
2. **I don't like to eat any kind of fish for breakfast.**
   kind of fish / to eat any / I don't like / for breakfast
3. **Mark made some pasta with tomatoes, olive oil, and cheese.**
   and cheese / tomatoes, olive oil, / Mark made / some pasta with
4. **He ate a salad of lettuce and tomatoes with cheese on top.**
   with cheese / He ate a / lettuce and tomatoes / salad of / on top
5. **We don't have any butter, yogurt, or cheese in the refrigerator.**
   any butter, yogurt, / We don't have / refrigerator / or cheese / in the

3. Reading Comprehension Questions

Read again the paragraph above under Let's Practice 5. Listening Activity. Circle True or False.

1. True **False** Adam could eat fruit from any tree in the garden.
2. True **False** Adam could eat from the tree of knowledge.
3. **True** False Eve ate fruit from the tree of knowledge.
4. **True** False Noah could eat all green plants.
5. True **False** Noah could eat animals with blood in them.
6. True **False** We should eat all the honey we want.
7. True **False** Honey will make you sick.
8. **True** False Too much wine can make you poor.
9. True **False** You should eat from all five food groups every day.

2. Scrambled Sentence

Put the words of the sentences into correct order.

1. when you go / to the supermarket / Would you buy / some pasta / some rice and

___

2. kind of fish / to eat any / I don't like / for breakfast

___

3. and cheese / tomatoes, olive oil, / Mark made / some pasta with

___

4. with cheese / He ate a / lettuce and tomatoes / salad of / on top

___

5. any butter, yogurt, / We don't have / refrigerator / or cheese / in the

___

Listening Activity.

Circle True or False.

1. True False Adam could eat fruit from any tree in the garden.
2. True False Adam could eat from the tree of knowledge.
3. True False Eve ate fruit from the tree of knowledge.
4. True False Noah could eat all green plants.
5. True False Noah could eat animals with blood in them.
6. True False We should eat all the honey we want.
7. True False Honey will make you sick.
8. True False Too much wine can make you poor.
9. True False You should eat from all five food groups every day.

UNIT 4 – SHOPPING – LESSON 1 – I WENT SHOPPING TODAY
STUDENT BOOK PAGE 67

A. Prayer for Students & Self

B. Lesson Objective and Functions:
- Describing clothing by article, size, color

C. Grammar Structures:
- Past Tense Irregular Verbs

D. Biblical Reference or Principles:
- Mark 1:6

E. Materials & Preparation:

Introduce the colors by one of these methods:
- Pieces of construction paper
- Dry erase markers
- Crayons
- Internet images

<u>Introduction</u>

1. Ask: "Who likes to go shopping for clothing?" [get student responses]
2. Ask: "What things do you think about when choosing clothing? Size? Color? Article of clothing? Price?"
3. Say: "Today we are going to describe clothing by its size, color, article of clothing, and the price."
4. Point out the vocabulary box, but don't teach it from this page.

UNIT 4

SHOPPING

LESSON 1 – I WENT SHOPPING TODAY

Sizes	Colors		Articles of Clothing		Nouns	Verbs Past	
small	black	green	blouse	skirt	price tag	be	was/were
medium	blue	purple	necktie	suit		buy	bought
large	brown		pants			go	went
extra large	gray		shirt			spend	spent

UNIT 4 – SHOPPING – LESSON 1 – I WENT SHOPPING TODAY
STUDENT BOOK PAGE 68

Introduce New Vocabulary

1. Have students open to Unit 4 - Shopping; Lesson 1 – I Went Shopping Today.
2. Introduce the words or phrases with a repetition drill. For instruction on conducting repetition drills, see Activity Bank. Repeat each 5-6 times.
3. Elicit conversation by asking questions related to the articles of clothing.

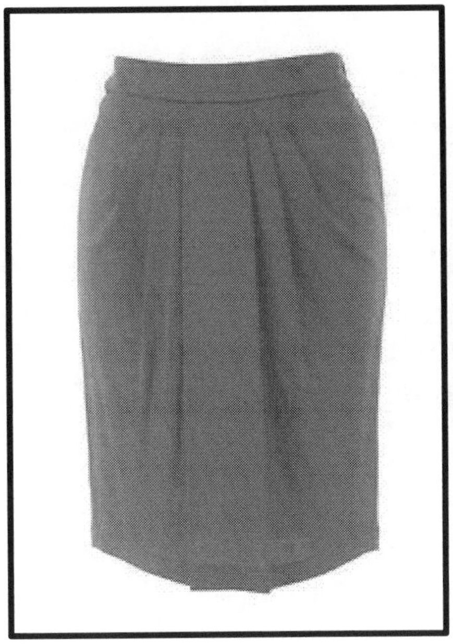

medium gray skirt

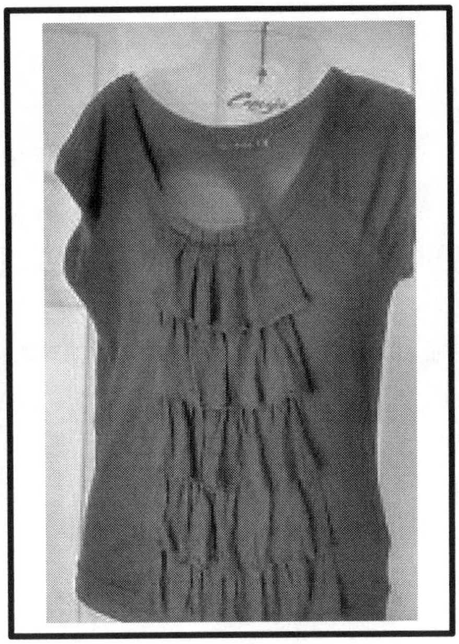

small purple blouse

large green shirt

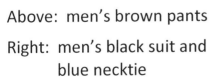

Above: men's brown pants

Right: men's black suit and blue necktie

UNIT 4 – SHOPPING – LESSON 1 – I WENT SHOPPING TODAY
STUDENT BOOK PAGE 69

Introduce the sizes with a repetition drill.

Elicit conversation regarding prices and survey students on their preferences for various clothing stores. Ask their opinions about price at the different stores they mention.

Although you may wish to introduce colors by using the students' clothing, you can't rely that all the colors you wish to introduce will be present in the room. Introduce the colors by one of these methods:

- Pieces of construction paper
- Dry erase markers
- Crayons
- Internet images

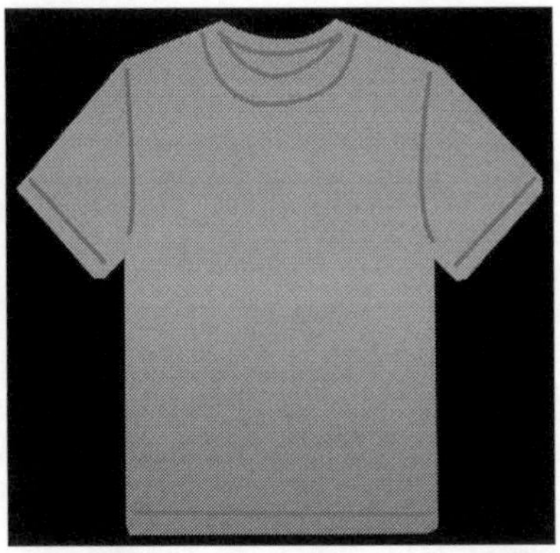

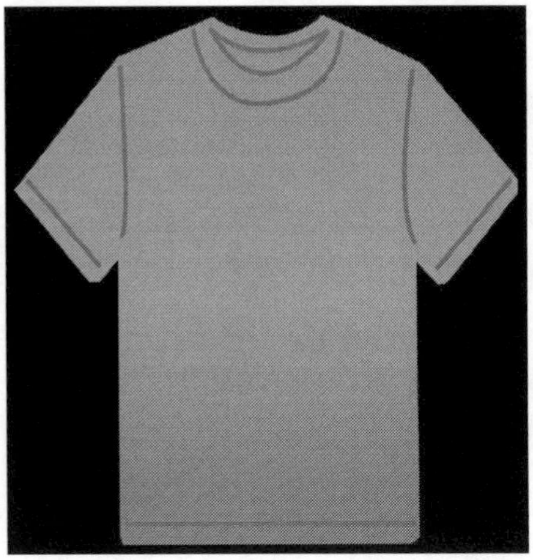

Sizes

Far Left: Small

Left: Medium

Bottom Left: Large

Bottom: Extra Large

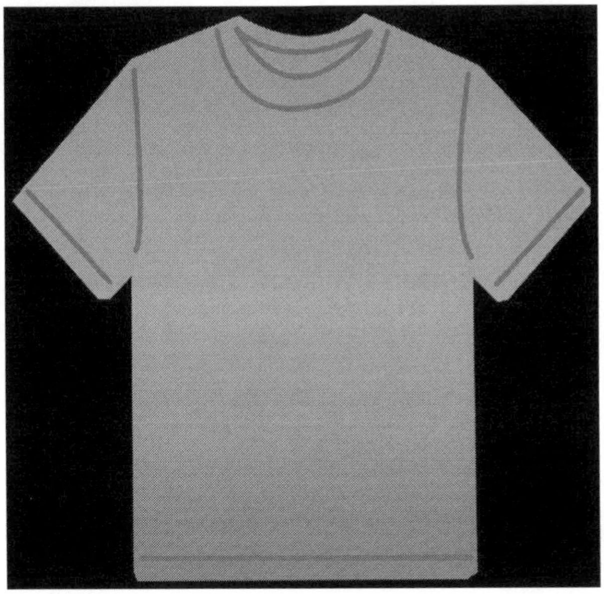

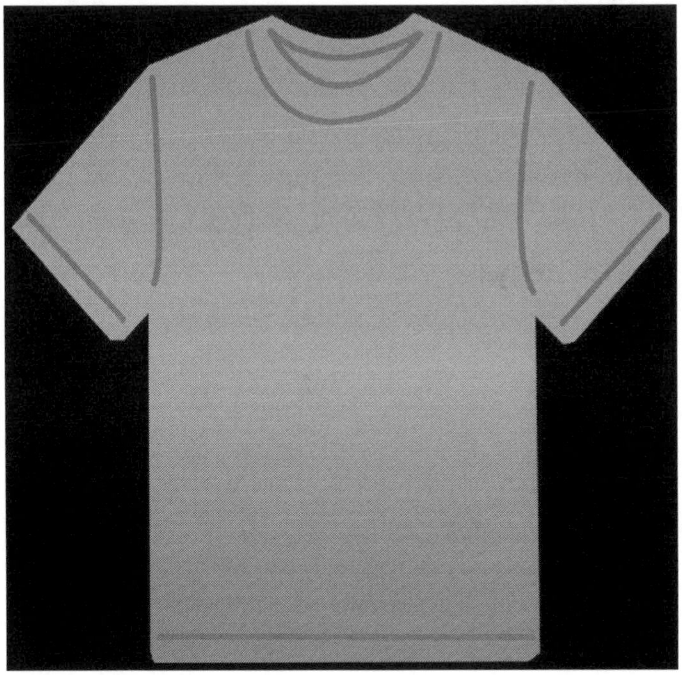

Colors

Gray	Brown
Green	Black
Purple	Blue

price tag

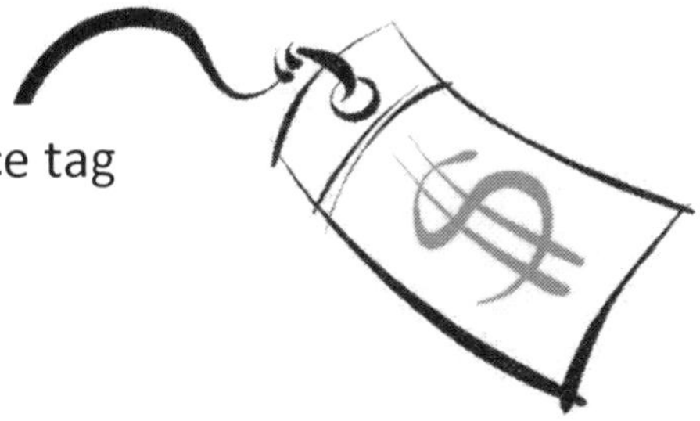

UNIT 4 – SHOPPING – LESSON 1 – I WENT SHOPPING TODAY
STUDENT BOOK PAGE 70

Time to Speak

A. Conversation I Went Shopping Today
   1. Ask: "Who are the 2 people in this conversation?"
   2. Have students complete *To Do First* by having students repeat each line after the instructor. Repeat each line 5-6 times. Strive for a normal conversational tone rather than an oral reading tone.
   3. Use backward build up for sentences longer than 4 words. Remember to divide sentences into sound units. See the Activity Bank for directions on backward build up and sound units.
   4. Use correct intonation, stress, and rhythm patterns. Include the following intonation patterns:
   - Statement (voice goes down at the end).
   - WH-Question (voice starts high on the WH-Question word, drops in the middle of the sentence, then goes up and down on the last word.)

B. Have students complete *To Do Second* and *To Do Third*.
Call on individual student pairs to read the conversations after each Substitution has been drilled. Volunteer pairs present conversations for the class.

Time to Speak

I Went Shopping Today

1.A. I went shopping today.

1.B. What did you buy?

2.A. I bought **a medium gray skirt** and **a small purple blouse.**

2.B. How much did you spend?

3.A. The skirt was $22.00 and **the blouse was $18.00.**

Substitution No. 1

1.A. I went shopping today.

1.B. What did you buy?

2.A. I bought **a large green shirt** and **an extra large pair of brown pants**.

2.B. How much did you spend?

3.A. The **shirt was $12.00** and the **pants were $27.00.**

Substitution No. 2

1.A. I went shopping today.

1.B. What did you buy?

2.A. I bought **a small black suit** and **a blue necktie**.

2.B. How much did you spend?

3.A. The **suit was $119.00** and the **necktie was $16.00**.

To Do First: Repeat the conversation after the instructor.

To Do Second: Speak with a partner. Change the underlined words in the conversation for the Substitutions.

To Do Third: Change partners. Talk about yourselves.

UNIT 4 – SHOPPING – LESSON 1 – I WENT SHOPPING TODAY
STUDENT BOOK PAGE 71

Grammar Foundation

1. Complete *To Do First* by having students read the information under Past Tense Irregular Verbs.
2. Have students complete *To Do Second* by having students repeat each example sentence after the instructor.
3. Ask for example sentences using the structures.
4. Repeat the procedure for the Word Order of Descriptive Adjectives.

Grammar Foundation

Past Tense Irregular Verbs - BE

- Many verbs form the past tense by adding -ED to the end of the verb. These are called Regular Past Tense Verbs. For example: waited, played, walked, talked, studied, cried, etc.
- Other verbs do not form the past tense by adding -ED. These are called Irregular Past Tense Verbs.
- There are several ways Irregular Verbs form the past tense.

(1) change the word - for example: sing - sang; do - did; have - had; go - went; eat - ate.

(2) use the same word - for example: put - put; hit - hit; hurt - hurt; cut - cut.

(3) use the same spelling, but different pronunciation - for example: read - read

Present Tense	Past Tense
BE Verb	
I am	I was
he Is	he was
ee are	we were
go	went
buy	bought
do	did

To Do First: Read the information about Past Tense Irregular Verbs BE.

To Do Second: Repeat the example sentences for the Past Tense Irregular Verbs - BE.

To Do Third: Read the information about the Word Order of Descriptive Adjectives.

To Do Fourth: Begin the exercises to put the adjectives into correct order.

Word Order of Descriptive Adjectives

DESCRIPTIVE ADJECTIVES are used to describe Nouns: persons, places, things. Adjectives come before Nouns in the normal English word order. Most Nouns are usually modified by only one or two Adjectives. Sometimes you will see three or more Adjectives before a Noun.

UNIT 4 – SHOPPING – LESSON 1 – I WENT SHOPPING TODAY
STUDENT BOOK PAGE 72

Begin the exercises to put the Adjectives and Noun into correct order. Do Nos. 1-2. Assign Nos. 3-5 for homework. Although it is not in the student text, help students formulate whole sentences with the Adjectives and Noun. For example: The kind, old Mexican woman was Monica's grandmother.

Put the Adjectives and the one Noun into correct order.

Example: Mexican, old, kind, woman	*kind, old, Mexican woman.*
1. red, large, cotton, beautiful, sweater	**beautiful, large, red cotton sweater**
2. silver, short, new, interesting, lamp	**interesting, short, new, silver lamp**
3. red, wonderful, tall, Chinese, flower	**wonderful, tall, red, Chinese flower**
4. little, Ecuadorian, red, old, dirty, bicycle	**dirty, little, old, red, Ecuadorian bicycle**
5. wonderful, old, tiny, metal, Haitian, bottle	**wonder, tiny, old, Haitian, metal bottle**

Practicing Perfect Pronunciation

Have students repeat the tongue twisters after the instructor.

1. great gray and green garage
2. a pretty pair of purple pants
3. small, medium, large, extra large
4. a beautiful blue, black, and brown blouse
5. some silky skirts, shirts, and suits

There are six different kinds of Adjectives including: opinion, size, age, color, nationality, and material. When we have more than one Adjective modifying a Noun, the Adjectives follow a certain word order. That word order is as listed below.

(1) opinion - adjectives that express a personal opinion such as rich, beautiful, happy, ugly.

(2) size - small, medium, large, etc.

(3) age - 25 years old, young, middle aged, etc.

(4) color - red, black, dark, light, etc.

(5) nationality - American, Haitian, Cuban, Chinese, Colombian, Indian, etc.

(6) material - adjectives that describe what a noun is made of such as fabric, steel, paper, wood, plastic, etc.

Put the Adjectives and the one Noun into correct order.

Example: Mexican, old, kind, woman ***kind, old, Mexican woman.***

1. red, large, cotton, beautiful, sweater ____________________

____

2. silver, short, new, interesting, lamp ____________________

____

3. red, wonderful, tall, Chinese, flower ____________________

____

4. little, Ecuadorian, red, old, dirty, bicycle ____________________

____

5. wonderful, old, tiny, metal, Haitian, bottle ____________________

____

~~Practicing Perfect Pronunciation~~

Repeat the tongue twisters after the instructor.

1. great gray and green garage
2. a pretty pair of purple pants
3. small, medium, large, extra large
4. a beautiful blue, black, and brown blouse
5. some silky skirts, shirts, and suits

UNIT 4 – SHOPPING – LESSON 1 – I WENT SHOPPING TODAY
STUDENT BOOK PAGE 73

Let's Practice

A. Conduct the Let's Practice Activity 1. Play Change the Chair

1. Have students form a large circle with chairs facing inward.
2. Demonstrate. Student 1 does not have a chair, so have Student 1 stand in the center of the circle with the instructor. The instructor tells Student 1 to give a command, for example: "Everyone wearing red color change your chair."
3. All students wearing red color must stand and change to a different chair while Student 1 also takes one of the vacated chairs.
4. The student without a chair gives the next command.

B. Conduct the Let's Practice Activity 2. Interview Line-Up

For instructions on how to set up and conduct an Interview Line-Up, see Activity Bank. Ask these questions:

1. What is your favorite store to shop for clothing? Why?
2. Describe your favorite T-shirt. What's it look like? Why is it your favorite?
3. Would you borrow money to pay for a wedding dress or suit? Why or why not?
4. Do you know anyone who has their clothing made by a dressmaker? Which articles of clothing do they have made?
5. What are your favorite colors for clothing? Why?
6. Which color would you NOT wear in clothing? Why not?

C. Conduct the Let's Practice Activity 3. Reading for Information

Instructor reads the passage at a normal speed while students follow along silently.

1. After reading a short time, the instructor will ask questions about the passage. See the questions after each section.
2. When finished, instructor may ask the students to read the passage, each student reading a few lines.

Back to School Shopping

By Barbara Kinney Black

Maria's children needed new clothes for school. So, Maria went shopping. For Shawn she bought a small pair of blue jeans and a small red T-shirt. For Timmy she found two pairs of medium pants – one pair was brown and the other pair was gray – and she found two long-sleeved shirts – one purple and one white.

Let's Practice

1. Play Change the Chair

1. Students form a large circle with chairs facing inward.
2. Student 1 does not have a chair so Student 1 stands in the center of the circle. Student 1 gives a command, for example: "Everyone wearing red color change your chair."
3. All students wearing red color must stand and change to a different chair while Student 1 also takes a chair.
4. The student without a chair gives the next command.

2. Interview Line-Up

1. Follow the instructor's directions. Make a line with other students.
2. Ask questions to other students. The instructor will give you the questions.

3. Reading for Information

1. The instructor will read the passage. Follow along silently.
2. After reading a short time, the instructor will ask questions about the passage.

Back to School Shopping

By Barbara Kinney Black

Maria's children needed new clothes for school. So, Maria went shopping. For Shawn she bought a small pair of blue jeans and a small red T-shirt. For Timmy she found two pairs of medium pants – one pair was brown and the other pair was gray – and she found two long-sleeved shirts – one purple and one white.

Next, Maria went to a store for young girls where she got two skirts and three blouses for Julie. The skirts were size medium. One skirt was black and the other skirt was blue. Julie loves purple and pink, so Maria bought one purple blouse and one pink T-shirt. Maria also found a white blouse for Julie.

Finally, she went to a store for big and tall men. Her son, Ricardo, is 6 foot tall. The extra-large size is never big enough for Ricardo, but in the big and tall men's store, Maria found some black pants that were just the right size. She got two pairs for Ricardo. She also found an orange T-shirt and a green shirt. Maria was very happy with her purchases.

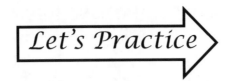

UNIT 4 – SHOPPING – LESSON 1 – I WENT SHOPPING TODAY
STUDENT BOOK PAGE 74

T/F	Shawn wears a size small pants and T-shirt	**true**
T/F	Maria bought two pairs of pants for Shawn	**false**
T/F	Maria bought two long-sleeved shirts	**true**

Next, Maria went to a store for young girls where she got two skirts and three blouses for Julie. The skirts were size medium. One skirt was black and the other skirt was blue. Julie loves purple and pink, so Maria bought one purple blouse and one pink T-shirt. Maria also found a white blouse for Julie.

T/F	Julie bought 3 blouses	**false**
T/F	Maria bought 2 skirts	**true**
T/F	Maria's favorite colors are purple and pink	**false**
T/F	Maria found a white blouse	**true**

Finally, she went to a store for big and tall men. Her son, Ricardo, is 6 foot tall. The extra-large size is never big enough for Ricardo, but in the big and tall men's store, Maria found some black pants that were just the right size. She got two pairs for Ricardo. She also found an orange T-shirt and a green shirt. Maria was very happy with her purchases.

T/F	Ricardo is 6 foot tall	**true**
T/F	Maria bought extra-large black pants	**false**
T/F	Maria found a green skirt	**false**

D. Conduct the Let's Practice Activity 4. Scrambled Spelling

1. Have students work with a small group to unscramble the spelling of the underlined words. Write the correct word on the line.
2. Students read the paragraph to the class.
3. NOTE: This is the Biblical principle. Instructor may wish to comment on the passage. **Teacher Answer Key in Bold**

In Mark 1:6 we [**read** d a e r] about the [**clothing** g n i h t o l c] of John the Baptist: "John [**wore** r o w e] clothing made of camel's [**hair** r a i h], with a leather belt [**around** r u d a o n] his waist, and he ate locusts and wild [**honey** y o h e n].

4. Scrambled Spelling

1. Work with a small group.
2. Read the paragraph below.
3. Unscramble the spelling of the underlined words. Write the correct word on the line.
4. Read your paragraph to the class.

In Mark 1:6 we [**d a e r** ________] about the [**g n i h t o l c** ________] of John the Baptist: "John [**r o w e** ________] clothing made of camel's [**r a i h** ________], with a leather belt [**r u d a o n** ________] his waist, and he ate locusts and wild [**y o h e n** ________]."

Left: camel Above: honey

Review Exercises

1. Write Sentences

Use the clothing words. Size is first. Color is second. Clothing is third.

1. red / skirt / medium ***I have a medium red skirt.***
2. blouse / purple / small ________
3. a pair of pants / brown / large ________

UNIT 4 – SHOPPING – LESSON 1 – I WENT SHOPPING TODAY
STUDENT BOOK PAGE 75

Review Exercises

Assign the Review Exercises for homework. Go over the instructions to ensure students understand how to complete each activity. **Answer Key in Bold**

1. Write Sentences

Use the clothing words. Size is first. Color is second. Clothing is third.

1. red / skirt / medium ***I have a medium red skirt.***
2. blouse / purple / small **small purple blouse**
3. a pair of pants / brown / large **large brown pair of pants**
4. shirt / large / green **large green shirt**
5. extra large / T-shirt / blue **extra large blue T-shirt**

2. Hidden Word Puzzle

Circle the words in the puzzle.

GREEN	PURPLE	GRAY	BROWN	BLACK	BLUE
SHIRT	SKIRT	SUIT	PANTS	BOUGHT	WENT

N K H K E W O J E S A T U S N K L Q I U W E O P Y U B V C X R P

A S D F G H K L N M B S D F G S A P Q I D **P A N T S** N I U Y T R

E W Q K L K J H H G F **G R E E N** D S S A W N T O N M B V C X D E

N I O N W T Q J T H E M N I O P W N J N K L N I N E T N E L N D

G N X T C X T T R M N N I O P Y T N B G F M I V Y F A **G R A Y** G

E W Q U Y T R N B J A S **B O U G H T** M J F A T U N H E R N K O Q

W N K T N A N K E W Q O U B R N I Q W N E I **P U R P L E** B T E W

Q I Y W I C X S I N Q W E R R B N V C Q N I Y T R E Q N I O N W

T A L O H **S H I R T** W A N Y S N I Y I O W T N Q I O U Y T H N K

A T N N I **B R O W N** U Y E N M L W O N T E W Q N V J A L N Q W E

R T Y I O P N K H G E N H H A Z I S W T I Y N I W T R W O R T R

S K I R T K N N T N N I I O Y Y I I N I E T G D A B N I N E N B

X O N Q W E R T F R D E W B N I N O I N O T **W E N T** E N I W O T

O A S V T N I N K H I Y E N S **B L A C K** T T H I M E S Q W E R T

Y U I O B M T T T N I N D A L S Y N I Y R T W Q N M B X B V W T

N I S E T D W T I Y O W E N A I Y I O P T A N D D I X X V B C Y

U O **S U I T** N I Q T Y G A I X S S G T O T E X B Q B N J S B D A

C B N K G N W Z T A B E N I T O K **B L U E** O A M N S G N K H G B

D A K W I N G O N A B C E G H T G F D S A N K O Y A Q E N T P I

C N G I N A M I Y N B E T Q T N I O W O R C O K I N G N I Y N T

4. shirt / large / green

5. extra large / T-shirt / blue

2. Hidden Word Puzzle

Circle the words in the puzzle.

GREEN	PURPLE	GRAY	BROWN	BLACK	BLUE
SHIRT	SKIRT	SUIT	PANTS	BOUGHT	WENT

```
N K H K E W O J E S A T U S N K L Q I U W E O P Y U B V C X R P
A S D F G H K L N M B S D F G S A P Q I D P A N T S N I U Y T R
E W Q K L K J H H G F G R E E N D S S A W N T O N M B V C X D E
N I O N W T Q J T H E M N I O P W N J N K L N I N E T N E L N D
G N X T C X T T R M N N I O P Y T N B G F M I V Y F A G R A Y G
E W Q U Y T R N B J A S B O U G H T M J F A T U N H E R N K O Q
W N K T N A N K E W Q O U B R N I Q W N E I P U R P L E B T E W
Q I Y W I C X S I N Q W E R R B N V C Q N I Y T R E Q N I O N W
T A L O H S H I R T W A N Y S N I Y I O W T N Q I O U Y T H N K
A T N N I B R O W N U Y E N M L W O N T E W Q N V J A L N Q W E
R T Y I O P N K H G E N H H A Z I S W T I Y N I W T R W O R T R
S K I R T K N N T N N I I O Y Y I I N I E T G D A B N I N E N B
X O N Q W E R T F R D E W B N I N O I N O T W E N T E N I W O T
O A S V T N I N K H I Y E N S B L A C K T T H I M E S Q W E R T
Y U I O B M T T T N I N D A L S Y N I Y R T W Q N M B X B V W T
N I S E T D W T I Y O W E N A I Y I O P T A N D D I X X V B C Y
U O S U I T N I Q T Y G A I X S S G T O T E X B Q B N J S B D A
C B N K G N W Z T A B E N I T O K B L U E O A M N S G N K H G B
D A K W I N G O N A B C E G H T G F D S A N K O Y A Q E N T P I
C N G I N A M I Y N B E T Q T N I O W O R C O K I N G N I Y N T
```

UNIT 4 – SHOPPING – LESSON 2 – BLACK FRIDAY SHOPPING
STUDENT BOOK PAGE 76

A. Prayer for Students & Self

B. Lesson Objective and Functions:
   - Identifying types of stores and products available

C. Grammar Structures:
   - Using BE GOING TO for Future

D. Biblical Reference or Principles:
   - Ephesians 2:8-9 For it is by grace you have been saved, through faith—and this is not from yourselves, it is the gift of God—not by works, so that no one can boast.

E. Materials & Preparation:
   - For the Let's Practice Activity 2. Mix 'n Match prepare 3x5 card sets with sentence halves. See further instruction under B. Conduct the Let's Practice Activity 2. Mix 'n Match.

<u>Introduction</u>

1. Ask: "What is Black Friday shopping?"
2. Instructor tells any experiences you have had with Black Friday shopping.
3. Ask for students' experiences with Black Friday shopping.
4. Poll the class for their opinions about Black Friday shopping. In general, do student like or dislilke the event? Do not go into too much detail here as the subject will be one of the Let's Practice activities more indepth.
5. Say: "Today we are going to learn about Black Friday shopping and the types of stores and products you can find in different stores."

Point out the vocabulary box, but don't teach it from this page **<u>except</u>** for the Nouns: Black Friday and crowds. Teach both these with a Repetition drill.

UNIT 4
SHOPPING

LESSON 2 – BLACK FRIDAY SHOPPING

Types of Stores		Products	Nouns
clothing store		board games	poinsettia plant
craft store	mall	Christmas decorations	Black Friday
dollar store	supermarket	clothing	crowds
drug store	toy store	gift cards	
garden center		jewelry making supplies	
Internet		perfume and cologne	

UNIT 4 – SHOPPING – LESSON 2 – BLACK FRIDAY SHOPPING
STUDENT BOOK PAGE 77

Introduce New Vocabulary

1. Have students open to Unit 4 - Shopping; Lesson 2 – Black Friday Shopping.
2. Introduce the words or phrases with a repetition drill. For instruction on conducting repetition drills, see Activity Bank. Repeat each 5-6 times.
3. Elicit conversation about the vocabulary by asking questions, for example:

- “Can you name the craft stores and supermarkets in our neighborhood?”
- “Have you bought or received gift cards? What are your favorite ones to receive?”
- “Do you or someone you know like to make crafts? What kind of crafts do you do?”

craft store

jewelry making supplies

supermarket

gift cards

UNIT 4 – SHOPPING – LESSON 2 – BLACK FRIDAY SHOPPING
STUDENT BOOK PAGE 78

1. Continue introducing stores and products with the repetition drill.
2. Continue eliciting conversation by asking related questions.

toy store

board games

drug store

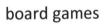

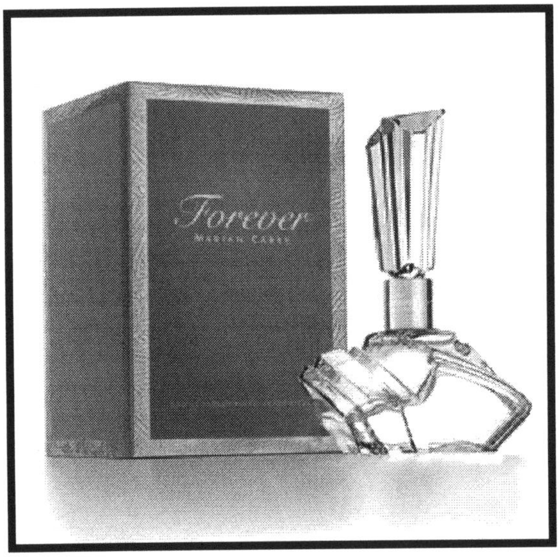

perfume and cologne

UNIT 4 – SHOPPING – LESSON 2 – BLACK FRIDAY SHOPPING
STUDENT BOOK PAGE 79

1. Continue introducing stores and products with the repetition drill.
2. Continue eliciting conversation by asking related questions.

dollar store

Christmas decorations

garden center

poinsettia plant

UNIT 4 – SHOPPING – LESSON 2 – BLACK FRIDAY SHOPPING
STUDENT BOOK PAGE 80

1. Continue introducing stores and products with the repetition drill.
2. Continue eliciting conversation by asking related questions.

Ask: "Do you shop on the Internet? Why or why not? What kinds of products do you purchase from the Internet?"

Left: clothing store

Above: mall

Stay home and shop on the Internet

UNIT 4 – SHOPPING – LESSON 2 – BLACK FRIDAY SHOPPING
STUDENT BOOK PAGE 81

Time to Speak

A. Conversation Black Friday Shopping
1. Ask: "Who are the 2 people in this conversation?"
2. Have students complete *To Do First* by having students repeat each line after the instructor. Repeat each line 5-6 times. Strive for a normal conversational tone rather than an oral reading tone.
3. Use backward build up for sentences longer than 4 words. Remember to divide sentences into sound units. See the Activity Bank for directions on backward build up and sound units.
4. Use correct intonation, stress, and rhythm patterns. Include the following intonation patterns:

- Statement (voice goes down at the end).
- YES/NO Question (voice goes up on the end).
- WH-Question (voice starts high, drops in the middle of the sentence, then up and down on the last word).

B. Have students complete *To Do Second*.
Call on individual student pairs to read the conversations after each Substitution has been drilled. Volunteer pairs present conversations for the class.

C. Have students complete *To Do Third* by changing partners and using the conversation as a guide to create their own conversations about Black Friday shopping.

Time to Speak

Black Friday Shopping

1.A. Are you going to go Christmas shopping on Black Friday?

1.B. Oh, yes. I'm going to go to the **craft store** for some **jewelry making supplies**. What about you?

2.A. I don't like the crowds, so I'm going to go to the **supermarket**.

2.B. The **supermarket**? What will you buy there?

3.A. **Gift cards** for everyone.

3.B. Oh, that sounds like a good idea!

Substitution No. 1

1.A. Are you going to go Christmas shopping on Black Friday?

1.B. Oh, yes. I'm going to go to the **toy store** for some **games**. What about you?

2.A. I don't like the crowds, so I'm going to go to the **drug store**.

2.B. The **drug store**? What will you buy there?

3.A. **Perfume and cologne** for everyone.

3.B. Oh, that sounds like a good idea!

To Do First: Repeat the conversation after the instructor.

To Do Second: Speak with a partner. Change the underlined words for the Substitutions.

To Do Third: Talk about yourselves.

Substitution No. 2

1.A. Are you going to go Christmas shopping on Black Friday?

1.B. Oh, yes. I'm going to go to the **dollar store** for some **Christmas decorations**. What about you?

2.A. I don't like the crowds, so I'm going to go to the **garden center**.

2.B. The **garden center**? What will you buy there?

UNIT 4 – SHOPPING – LESSON 2 – BLACK FRIDAY SHOPPING
STUDENT BOOK PAGE 82

Conclude Substitution Nos. 2 and 3.

Grammar Foundation

1. Complete *To Do First* by having students read the information under Using BE GOING TO to Express Future Plans.
2. Have students complete *To Do Second* by having students repeat each example sentence after the instructor.
3. Ask for example sentences using the structures.
4. Point out the NOTE about when the Main Verb is GO. Practice using GO as the Main Verb in additional statements. Have students make example statements.

3.A. **Christmas poinsettia plants** for everyone.

3.B. Oh, that sounds like a good idea!

Substitution No. 3

1.A. Are you going to go Christmas shopping on Black Friday?

1.B. Oh, yes. I'm going to go to the **mall** for some **clothing**. What about you?

2.A. I don't like the crowds, so I'm going to **shop on the Internet**.

2.B. The **Internet**? What will you buy there?

3.A. **Everything I want**.

3.B. Oh, that sounds like a good idea!

Grammar Foundation

Using BE GOING TO to Express Future Plans

To Do First: Read the information about the grammar structure.

To Do Second: Repeat examples.

Be Going To is used to express our future plans.

Subject + Be Verb + Going To + Main Verb

I	am	going to	go	to the craft store.
You	are	going to	go	to the mall.
He	is	going to	buy	some clothes.
She	is	going to	eat	lunch at 12:00.
We	are	going to	go	to the garden center.
They	are	going to	shop	at the drug store.

NOTE: It is important when the Main Verb is GO to include the verb in your statement. Many times you will hear for the Future someone say:

"I am going to the mall."

This statement is actually the Present Progressive for action at the present moment. In the grammar structure "BE GOING TO" is used to express the future. The Main Verb tells what the speaker is going to do in the future.

UNIT 4 – SHOPPING – LESSON 2 – BLACK FRIDAY SHOPPING
STUDENT BOOK PAGE 83

Grammar Foundation Continued…

5. Begin the exercise Complete the Sentences with the Words in Brackets by doing Nos. 1.-4. as a class.
6. Go over student responses.
7. Assign Nos. 4-10 as homework.

Practicing Perfect Pronunciation

Practice pronunciation of the reduced form 'gonna' for going to.

Complete the Sentences with the Words in Brackets

Use the words in the brackets to complete the sentence. Use all the words. Use BE GOING TO for Future.

[I, go, mall] ***I am going to go to the mall.***

1. [he, buy, books] ______
2. [she, get, Christmas decorations] ______
3. [we, go, supermarket] ______
4. [they, shop, Internet] ______
5. [I, play, board games] ______
6. [She, buy, jewelry making supplies] ______
7. [We, get, gift cards] ______
8. [She, buy, poinsettia plants] ______
9. [He, go, drug store] ______
10. [They, buy, perfume and cologne] ______

~~*Practicing Perfect Pronunciation*~~

When English is spoken quickly, the words 'going to' are reduced to sound like "gonna". Repeat this reduction after the instructor.

UNIT 4 – SHOPPING – LESSON 2 – BLACK FRIDAY SHOPPING
STUDENT BOOK PAGE 84

Let's Practice

A. Conduct the Let's Practice Activity 1. Add On Game

1. Have students put the Products into alphabetical (A-Z) order on the board. Next to each Product, write the Type of Store where you can get that Product, for example: board games – toy store.
2. Student 1 makes a statement, for example: "I'm going to go to the toy store to buy some board games."
3. Student 2 repeats Student 1's statement and adds the next product listed on the board, for example, "I'm going to go to the toy store to buy some board games, and to the dollar store to buy some Christmas decorations."
4. Student 3 repeats Student 1 and 2's statements and adds the next type of store and product from the list on the board.
5. Continue repeating and adding stores and products until all have participated.

B. Conduct the Let's Practice Activity 2. Mix 'n Match

1. Prepare card matches in advance. On 3x5 cards write sentence halves as follows.

• I am going to go to the drug store	to buy some perfume.
• I am going to go to the dollar store	to buy some Christmas decorations.
• I am going to go to the supermarket	to buy some gift cards.
• I am going to go to the craft store	to buy some jewelry making supplies.
• I am going to go to the garden center	to buy some poinsettia plants.
• I am going to go to the toy store	to buy some board games.
• I am going to go to the clothing store	to buy some clothes.

2. Distribute cards randomly to students.
3. Students mix with each other to find the other half of their sentences.
4. Students read their completed matches to the class.

C. Conduct the Let's Practice Activity 3. Answer Questions about the Conversation

1. Have students go back to the conversation "Black Friday Shopping."
2. Ask the following questions. Students will respond silently by writing their answers in their books.

Let's Practice

1. Add On Game

1. Students put the Products into alphabetical (A-Z) order on the board. Next to each Product, write the Type of Store where you can get that Product, for example: board games – toy store.
2. Student 1 makes a statement, for example: "I'm going to go to the toy store to buy some board games."
3. Student 2 repeats Student 1's statement and adds the next product listed on the board, for example, "I'm going to go to the toy store to buy some board games, and to the dollar store to buy some Christmas decorations."
4. Student 3 repeats Student 1 and 2's statements and adds the next type of store and product from the list on the board.
5. Continue repeating and adding stores and products until all have participated.

2. Mix 'n Match

1. The instructor will give students a card. Each card has part of a sentence.
2. Mix with each other to find the other half of your sentence.
3. Read your sentences to the class.

3. Answer Questions about the Conversation

1. Look at the conversation "Black Friday Shopping."

2. The instructor will ask some True/False questions. Do not say the answer. Look in the conversation and substitutions for the answer. Write your answers on the lines.

3. Go over your responses with the class.

1. ***true***	4. ______
2. ______	5. ______
3. ______	6. ______

UNIT 4 – SHOPPING – LESSON 2 – BLACK FRIDAY SHOPPING
STUDENT BOOK PAGE 85

3. Repeat each question 3-4 times while students look for the answer and write their responses.
4. Go over student responses with the class.

Questions

1.	T/F	You can buy jewelry making supplies at the craft store.	**true**
2.	T/F	You can't get perfume and cologne at the drug store.	**false**
3.	T/F	You can buy Christmas poinsettia plants at the mall.	**false**
4.	T/F	You can buy everything on the Internet.	**true**
5.	T/F	You can buy gift cards at the supermarket.	**true**
6.	T/F	You can't buy clothing at the mall.	**false**

D. Conduct the Let's Practice Activity 4. Survey

1. Instructor demonstrates. Write the two questions on the board:
   Do you like to go Black Friday shopping?
   What kinds of products do you buy for Christmas?
2. Ask Student 1, "Do you like to go Black Friday shopping?" Write his/her response on the board.
3. Ask the second question and write the response on the board.
4. Have students talk to their classmates. Ask the questions and write their classmate's responses on their surveys.
5. Go over student responses with the class.

E. Conduct the Let's Practice Activity 5. Scrambled Spelling

NOTE: This is the Biblical principle. Instructor may wish to comment on the verse when finished. **Teacher Answer Key in Bold**

1. Have students work with a small group to unscramble the spelling of the underlined words.
2. Students write the correct word on the line next to the scrambled spelling.
3. Students read the completed paragraph to the class.

Ephesians 2:8-9 For it is by [**grace** a c e g r __________] you have been saved, through [**faith** h i t a f __________]—and this is not from [**yourselves** o r e v s y u s l e __________], it is the [**gift** t l g f __________] of God—not by [**works** s o k r w __________], so that no one can boast.

4. Survey

1. Talk to your classmates. Ask questions:
   - "Do you like to go Black Friday shopping?"
   - "What kinds of products do you buy for Christmas?"
2. Write their responses on your survey, for example: "John buys gift cards and board games."

Name	Do you like to go Black Friday shopping?	What kinds of products do You buy for Christmas?
Barbara	***no***	***gift cards, candy, clothing***

5. Scrambled Spelling

1. Work with a small group.
2. Read the paragraph below.
3. Unscramble the spelling of the underlined words. Write the correct word on the line.
4. Read your paragraph to the class.

Ephesians 2:8-9 For it is by [a c e g r __________] you have been saved, through [h i t a f __________]—and this is not from [o r e v s y u s l e __________], it is the [t l g f __________] of God—not by [s o k r w __________], so that no one can boast.

UNIT 4 – SHOPPING – LESSON 2 – BLACK FRIDAY SHOPPING
STUDENT BOOK PAGE 86

Review Exercises

Assign the Review Exercises for homework. Go over the instructions to ensure students understand how to complete each activity. **Answer Key in Bold**

1. Choose the Correct Word

In each of the [brackets] below you will find two of the new vocabulary words. Circle the word that best completes the sentence.

1. I don't like [**crowds** / Christmas decorations] so I'm going to shop on the Internet.
2. Joe is [going / **going to go**] to the drug store to buy some perfume.
3. Amy [is going / **went**] to the supermarket and bought gift cards.
4. Gladys [go / **is going to go**] to the garden center.
5. Monica always [**goes** / going] to the toy store for Christmas every year.
6. Is Carmen [**going to go** / went] to the craft store for jewelry making supplies?

2. What's the Next Line?

Read the statements. You will find two responses. Circle the correct response.

1. I'm going to go to the garden center.
A. What are you going to buy? B. I'm going to buy poinsettia plants.
2. Joe bought gift cards for Christmas.
A. Where did he buy them? B. I am going to go to the toy store.
3. Where can I buy some perfume and cologne?
A. You can buy some jewelry making supplies. **B. You can buy them in the drug store.**
4. What can you buy on the Internet?
A. Mom bought some board games for Christmas. **B. You can buy anything on the Internet.**
5. Where do you buy Christmas decorations?
A. I don't buy gift cards for Christmas. **B. I buy decorations at the dollar store.**
6. Mom always buys Christmas decorations.
A. Where does she buy them? B. Mom always shops on the Internet.

Review Exercises

1. Choose the Correct Word

In each of the [brackets] below you will find two of the new vocabulary words.
Circle the word that best completes the sentence.

1. I don't like [crowds / Christmas decorations] so I'm going to shop on the Internet.
2. Joe is [going / going to go] to the drug store to buy some perfume.
3. Amy [is going / went] to the supermarket and bought gift cards.
4. Gladys [go / is going to go] to the garden center.
5. Monica always [goes / going] to the toy store for Christmas every year.
6. Is Carmen [going to go / went] to the craft store for jewelry making supplies?

2. What's the Next Line?

Read the statements. You will find two responses. Circle the correct response.

1. I'm going to go to the garden center.

A. What are you going to buy? B. I'm going to buy poinsettia plants.

2. Joe bought gift cards for Christmas.

A. Where did he buy them? B. I am going to go to the toy store.

3. Where can I buy some perfume and cologne?

A. You can buy some jewelry making supplies. B. You can buy them in the drug store.

4. What can you buy on the Internet?

A. Mom bought some board games for Christmas. B. You can buy anything on the Internet.

5. Where do you buy Christmas decorations?

A. I don't buy gift cards for Christmas. B. I buy decorations at the dollar store.

6. Mom always buys Christmas decorations.

A. Where does she buy them? B. Mom always shops on the Internet.

UNIT 5 – HOUSING – LESSON 1 – MOVING IN
STUDENT BOOK PAGE 87

A. Prayer for Students & Self

B. Lesson Objective and Functions:
   - Describing placement of furnishings in rooms

C. Grammar Structures:
   - Imperative Commands using Demonstratives

D. Biblical Reference or Principles:
   - Luke 9:58

<u>Introduction</u>

1. Ask: "What do you see in the picture?" [men moving furniture]
2. Ask: "How do you move? Do you hire a moving company or move yourself?"
3. Say: "Today we are going to learn vocabulary for moving and arranging things in the different rooms of the house."

Point out the vocabulary box, but don't teach it from this page.

UNIT 5
HOUSING

LESSON 1 – MOVING IN

Rooms	Furnishings & Furniture			Prepositions of Location
bathroom	bed	night stand	table	across from
bedroom	chair	pictures	T.V.	in
kitchen	coffee table	pillows	T.V. stand	next to
living room	end table	sofa		on

UNIT 5 – HOUSING – LESSON 1 – MOVING IN
STUDENT BOOK PAGE 88

Introduce New Vocabulary

1. Have students open to Unit 5 – Housing; Lesson 1 – Moving In.
2. Introduce the words or phrases with a repetition drill. For instruction on conducting repetition drills, see Activity Bank. Repeat each 5-6 times.
3. Elicit conversation from students about the vocabulary by asking questions, such as:

- "Do you have a T.V. in your bedroom?"
- "What size bed do you prefer? Twin, Full, Queen, King?" NOTE: Instructor may wish to have the dimensions of each size on hand, should a student ask that question. It's easily acquired on the Internet.
- "How many pillows do you use for yourself?"

NOTE: The Preposition of Location ON is illustrated with the T.V. on the T.V. stand. Be sure to point this out. The other Prepositions of Location are taught two pages over.

master bedroom and bed

night stand

bed pillows

The T.V. is ON the T.V. stand

UNIT 5 – HOUSING – LESSON 1 – MOVING IN
STUDENT BOOK PAGE 89

1. Continue introducing vocabulary of rooms and furnishings with a repetition drill.
2. Continue eliciting conversation about pictures.

Living room
with:

sofa
coffee table
end table
chair

Put these pictures on the table

UNIT 5 – HOUSING – LESSON 1 – MOVING IN
STUDENT BOOK PAGE 90

1. Introduce the Prepositions of Location IN, NEXT TO, and ACROSS FROM using the pictues as illustrations.
2. NOTE: "Lizzy" is the stuffed lizard. The figure in the bottom picture is "Gumby." He is facing away from the viewers so that is his right arm that is extended out and his left arm pointing up.

NOTE: A reminder that the Preposition of Location ON was taught two pages ealier with the picture of the T.V. on the T.V. stand.

Lizzy is

IN

the box.

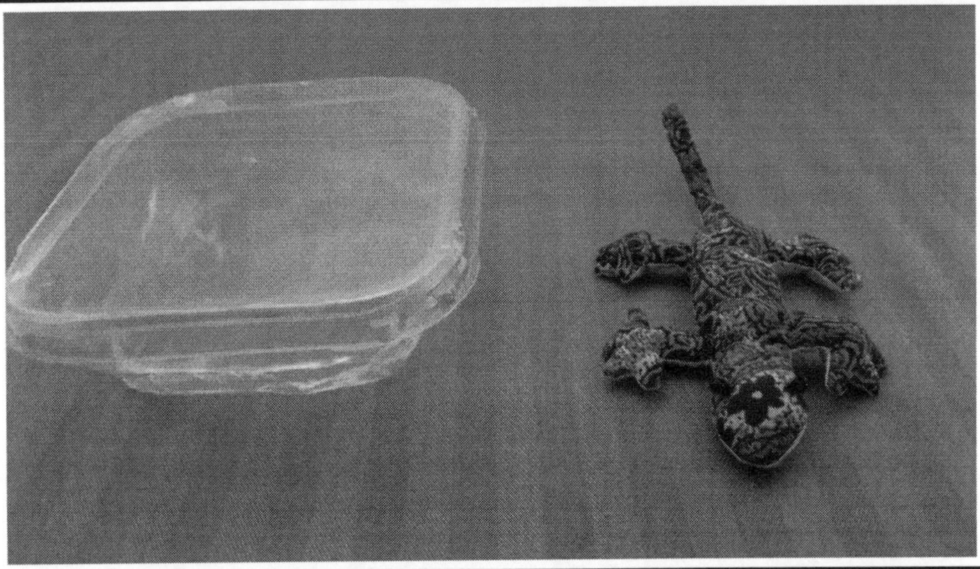

Lizzy is

NEXT TO

the box.

The Post Office is

ACROSS FROM

the church.

UNIT 5 – HOUSING – LESSON 1 – MOVING IN
STUDENT BOOK PAGE 91

1. Go over the floor plan identifying the room names.
2. Ask questions about the floor plan, including:

- Which room is larger: the living room or bedroom? [Students need to look at the dimensions to answer. It may be necessary to explain the measurement system.]
- How many closets are there? [2]
- How do you get to the bath? [through the bedroom]
- What fixture is in the kitchen? [sink]
- What fixtures are in the bath? [sink, shower, toilet]
- How many rooms are there? [6]

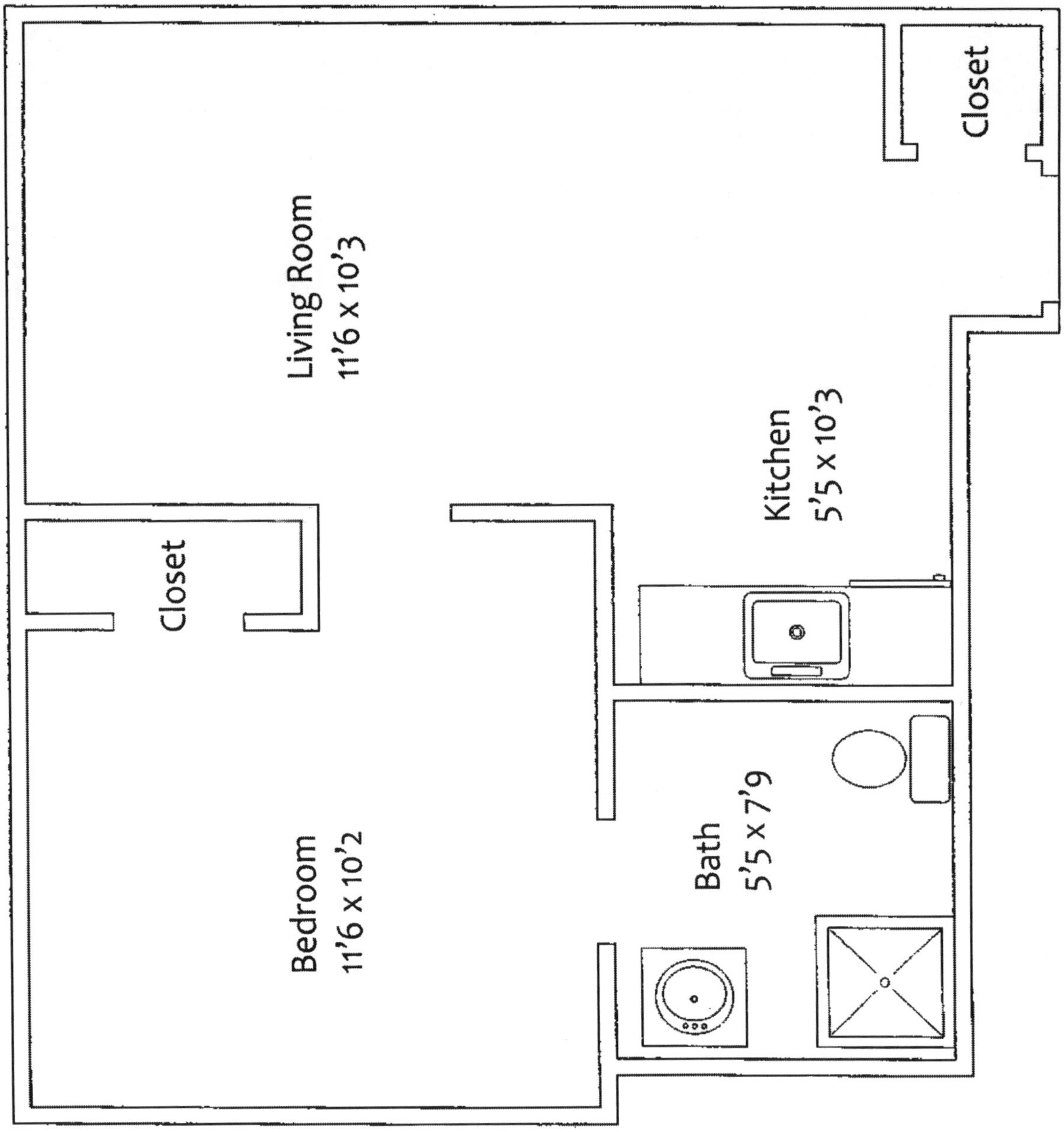
Closet
Living Room
11’6 x 10’3
Kitchen
5’5 x 10’3
Closet
Bath
5’5 x 7’9
Bedroom
11’6 x 10’2

UNIT 5 – HOUSING – LESSON 1 – MOVING IN
STUDENT BOOK PAGE 92

Time to Speak

A. Conversation Moving In

1. Ask: "Who are the 2 people in this conversation?"
2. Have students complete *To Do First* by having students repeat each line after the instructor. Repeat each line 5-6 times. Strive for a normal conversational tone rather than an oral reading tone.
3. Use backward build up for sentences longer than 4 words. Remember to divide sentences into sound units. See the Activity Bank for directions on backward build up and sound units.
4. Use correct intonation, stress, and rhythm patterns. Include the following intonation patterns:

- Statement (the voice starts higher and moves downward like going down a staircase through each sound unit in a statement. When the end of the statement is reached, at the period, the voice falls).
- WH-Question (The voice begins on a high note with the WH-Question word, then falls through the middle of the sentence until the last Content Word when the voice rises to accent the accented syllable in the last Content Word and then falls).

B. Have students complete *To Do Second* and *To Do Third*.
Call on individual student pairs to read the conversations after each Substitution has been drilled. Volunteer pairs present conversations for the class.

Time to Speak

Moving In

Speaker A: Home owner

Speaker B: Moving company employee

1.A. Please put **that bed in** the **master bedroom**.

1.B. Where do you want **this night stand**?

2.A. Put **that night stand next to** the **bed**.

2.B. Where do you want **these pillows**?

3.A. Put **those pillows on** the **bed**.

3.B. Where do you want **this TV**?

4.A. Put **that TV across from** the **bed**.

4.B. O.K.

To Do First: Repeat the conversation after the instructor.

To Do Second: Speak with a partner. Change the underlined words in the conversation for the Substitutions.

To Do Third: Change partners and repeat the Substitutions.

Substitution No. 1

1.A. Please put **that sofa in** the **living room**.

1.B. Where do you want **this table**?

2.A. Put **that table next to** the **sofa.**

2.B. Where do you want **these pictures**?

3.A. Put **those pictures on** the **table**.

3.B. Where do you want **this TV?**

4.A. Put **that TV across from** the **sofa.**

4.B. O.K.

UNIT 5 – HOUSING – LESSON 1 – MOVING IN
STUDENT BOOK PAGE 93

Grammar Foundation

1. Complete *To Do First* by having students read the information under Using Demonstratives – THIS, THAT, THESE, THOSE.
2. Have students complete *To Do Second* by having students repeat each example sentence after the instructor.
3. Ask for example sentences using the structures.
4. Repeat instructions to introduce Imperative Commands.

Grammar Foundation

Using DEMONSTRATIVES - THIS, THAT, THESE, THOSE

DEMONSTRATIVES are used with nouns to explain which Noun we are speaking about. THIS and THAT are used with Singular Nouns while THESE and THOSE are used with Plural Nouns.

- THIS is used when the Noun is in the speaker's possession or near to the speaker.
- THAT is used when the Noun is not in the speaker's possession or not near to the speaker.
- THESE is used when the plural Nouns are in the speaker's possession or near to the speaker.
- THOSE is used when the plural Nouns are not in the speaker's possession or near to the speaker.

Imperative Commands

Imperatives are used when you want to tell someone to do something such as commands, orders, instructions, or polite requests. In an Imperative sentence, use the base form of the verb.

Imperatives are often used without a subject in the sentence. For example:

- Stop!
- Open the door.
- Put the sofa next to the TV.
- Please come here.

The negative imperative uses DON'T.

- Don't talk to me.
- Don't watch TV.
- Don't put the bed in the bathroom.
- Please don't do that.

When you want someone to do something with you, use LET'S.

To Do First: Read the information about Demonstratives.

To Do Second: Repeat the example sentences after the instructor.

To Do Third: Repeat instructions for Imperative Commands.

UNIT 5 – HOUSING – LESSON 1 – MOVING IN
STUDENT BOOK PAGE 94

Practice Polite Imperative Commands

1. Play Simon Says.
2. Have students all stand up. Give a command for something they can do easily from where they are standing, for example: "Please pick up your pencil."
3. Direct students to respond by performing the action requested IF the instructor uses a Polite Imperative Command beginning with the word, 'Please'.
4. If the instructor does NOT use a Polite Imperative Command with Please, for example: "Pick up your pencil," students are NOT to respond by doing the action. Any student who DOES perform the action will be out and must sit down.
5. Continue giving Polite Imperative Commands with Please in rapid succession and now and then throw in a command without saying Please.
6. Continue eliminating students until only one remains standing.
7. Play as many rounds as you can afford the time.

NOTE: Popular commands are to touch various body parts, raise the hand, wave good-bye, touch your book, etc.

Practicing Perfect Pronunciation

Practice the sounds of /p/ and /th/ by having students repeat the tongue twisters after the instructor:

1. Please put the pictures and pillows in Pamela's room.
2. Theodore, Please put that T.V., those towels, that pillow, these teacups, and this picture in the trash. I don't want them anymore. Thanks, Theodore.

Let's Practice

A. Conduct the Let's Practice Activity 1. Cloze Dictation – Listening Activity

James and Joann Move In

By Barbara K. Black

James and Joann **bought** a new house. They are telling the moving company employee where to put their **furniture** in the new house. Joann says, "Please put that **bed i**nto the master **bedroom**. Also, please put those night stands **next to** the bed." James is helping to bring in a large **sofa**. Joann tells him to put it in the living room. The mover brings in a coffee table and **a chair**. Joann wants those in the living room, too. She wants the coffee table next to the sofa and the chair **across from** the coffee table. James has some pictures and **bed pillows** in his arms. Joann says, "Please put those **pictures** in the living room and put those pillows in the **bedroom**." The movers brought the last piece of

- Let's go to the park.
- Let's watch TV.
- Let's put the pictures on the wall.

In this lesson Imperative Commands are used as commands where to place items of furniture.

Practice Polite Imperative Commands

Students practice responding to polite Imperative Commands.

Follow the instructor's directions.

~~*Practicing Perfect Pronunciation*~~

Practice the sounds of /p/ and /th/ by repeating the tongue twisters after the instructor:

1. Please put the pictures and pillows in Pamela's room.
2. Theodore, please put that T.V., those towels, that pillow, these teacups, and this picture in the trash. I don't want them anymore. Thanks, Theodore.

Let's Practice

1. Cloze Dictation - Listening Activity

Listen to the instructor read the paragraph. Write the missing words on the lines.

James and Joann Move In

By Barbara K. Black

James and Joann ________________ a new house. They are telling the moving company employee where to put their _________________ in the new house. Joann says, "Please put that ________ into the master _________________. Also, please put those night stands ___________________ the bed." James is helping to bring in a large _________. Joann tells him to put it in the living room. The mover brings in a coffee table and _____. Joann wants those in the living room, too. She wants the coffee table next to the sofa and the chair ________________ the coffee table. James has some pictures and ___ _______________ in his arms. Joann says, "Please put those ________________ in the living room and put those pillows in the _____________." The movers brought the last

UNIT 5 – HOUSING – LESSON 1 – MOVING IN
STUDENT BOOK PAGE 95

furniture into the house—an **end table**. Joann decides she doesn't want that end table any more so she says, "Please **put** that end table **in** the trash." Now James and Joann's house looks nice.

B. Conduct the Let's Practice Activity 2. Pair, Square, Share

1. Pairs of students interview each other.
2. After both partners share, each pair then joins another pair to make a group of 4 (a square).
3. The original partners summarize their partner's responses to this group of 4.
4. Continue until all students have summarized their original partner's responses.
5. NOTE: If the activity is finished too quickly, form new groups and repeat.

C. Conduct the Let's Practice Activity 3. Place the Furniture in the Room – Pair Activity

1. Have students tear a piece of paper into 10 pieces.
2. Write one furnishing on each paper. Include: bed, pillows, night stand, T.V., T.V. stand, sofa, coffee table, end table, chair, pictures.
3. Have students open their books to the apartment floor plan.
4. Students work with a partner.
5. Instructor demonstrates: Student 1 is the moving company employee. Student 2 (Instructor) is the home owner. The home owner gives a command, for example: "Please put that sofa in the living room."
6. Student 1 takes his/her sofa paper and places into the living room on the floor plan. Student 2 continues to give commands to Student 1 until all furnishings have been placed on the floor plan.
7. Reverse roles and repeat.

D. Conduct the Let's Practice Activity 4. Play Beat the Cat

NOTE: This is the Biblical principle. The instructor may wish to comment on the passage.

1. Play Beat the Cat with this puzzle sentence: Luke 9:58b "but the Son of Man has no place to lay his head."
2. For instructions on how to set up and conduct Beat the Cat, see the Activity Bank.
3. After conclusion of the puzzle, reveal the beginning of the verse: "Jesus replied, 'Foxes have dens and birds have nests, but the Son of Man has no place to lay his head.'"

piece of furniture into the house—an ________________. Joann decides she doesn't want that end table any more so she says, "Please __________ that end table **in** the trash." Now James and Joann's house looks nice.

2. Pair, Square, Share

1. Work with a partner. Student 1 asks: "What furniture do you have in your living room?"
2. Student 2 answers.
3. Student 2 asks: "What furniture do you have in your bedroom?"
4. Student 1 answers.
5. When finished, listen for the instructor's instructions.

3. Place the Furniture in the Room – Pair Activity

1. Tear a piece of paper into 10 pieces.
2. Write one furnishing on each paper. Include: bed, pillows, night stand, T.V., T.V. stand, sofa, coffee table, end table, chair, pictures.
3. Open your book to the apartment floor plan.
4. Work with a partner. Student 1 is the moving company employee. Student 2 is the home owner.
5. The instructor will demonstrate.

4. Play Beat the Cat

1. This game is like the TV show Wheel of Fortune. The instructor will put a puzzle on the board.
2. Students take turns guessing consonants.
3. If the consonant is in the puzzle, the instructor will write it on the line. If the consonant is NOT in the puzzle, the instructor will draw part of a cat.
4. Continue until only vowels are left in the puzzle.

UNIT 5 – HOUSING – LESSON 1 – MOVING IN
STUDENT BOOK PAGE 96

Review Exercises

Assign the Review Exercises for homework. Go over the instructions to ensure students understand how to complete each activity. **Answer Key in Bold**

1. Write a Question for Each Statement

Write a question for each statement. Use the Demonstratives THIS, THAT, THESE and THOSE.

Where do you want these pictures?

Put those pictures in the bedroom.

1. ***Where do you want this chair?***

Put that chair in the living room.

2. ***Where do you want these pillows?***

Put those pillows in the bedroom.

3. ***Where do you want this T.V. and this T.V. stand?***

Please put that T.V. in the living room on that T.V. stand.

4. ***Where do you want this sofa and these night stands?***

Please put that sofa and those night stands in the master bedroom.

5. **Where do you want this brown end table and this black end table?**

Could you please put that brown end table in the living room and that black end table in the master bedroom?

2. Put the Conversation in Order

1. You will see the lines of a conversation. They are not in correct order.
2. Number the order of the lines of the conversation.

7 Yes, please put the end table next to the sofa.

1 James, I would like to rearrange the furniture.

Review Exercises

1. Write a Question for Each Statement

Write a question for each statement. Use the Demonstratives THIS, THAT, THESE and THOSE.

Where do you want these pictures?

Put those pictures in the bedroom.

1. ____________________

Put that chair in the living room.

2. ____________________

Put those pillows in the bedroom.

3. ____________________

Please put that T.V. in the living room on that T.V. stand.

4. ____________________

Please put that sofa and those night stands in the master bedroom.

____

5. ____________________

Could you please put that brown end table in the living room and that black end table in the master bedroom?

____

2. Put the Conversation in Order

1. You will see the lines of a conversation. They are not in correct order.
2. Number the order of the lines of the conversation.

__________Yes, please put the end table next to the sofa.

____1____James, I would like to rearrange the furniture.

__________O.K. Joann. Which room do you want to rearrange first?

__________O.K. Let's get started. Where do you want me to put this sofa?

__________First, I want to rearrange the living room.

__________Finally, would you put these pillows on the sofa?

__________I like the sofa by the window. Do you want me to put the end table next to the sofa?

__________Now second, would you please put this coffee table in front of the sofa?

__________Yes. I'll put the coffee table in front of the sofa.

__________Put that sofa by the window.________Sure. Those pillows look nice on the sofa. It looks like we are finished with the living room.

UNIT 5 – HOUSING – LESSON 1 – MOVING IN
STUDENT BOOK PAGE 96

_____**2**____O.K. Joann. Which room do you want to rearrange first?

_____**4**____O.K. Let's get started. Where do you want me to put this sofa?

_____**3**____First, I want to rearrange the living room.

_____**10**____Finally, would you put these pillows on the sofa?

_____**6**____I like the sofa by the window. Do you want me to put the end table next to the sofa?

_____**8**____Now second, would you please put this coffee table in front of the sofa?

_____**9**____Yes. I'll put the coffee table in front of the sofa.

_____**5**____Put that sofa by the window.

_____**11**____Sure. Those pillows look nice on the sofa. It looks like we are finished with the living room.

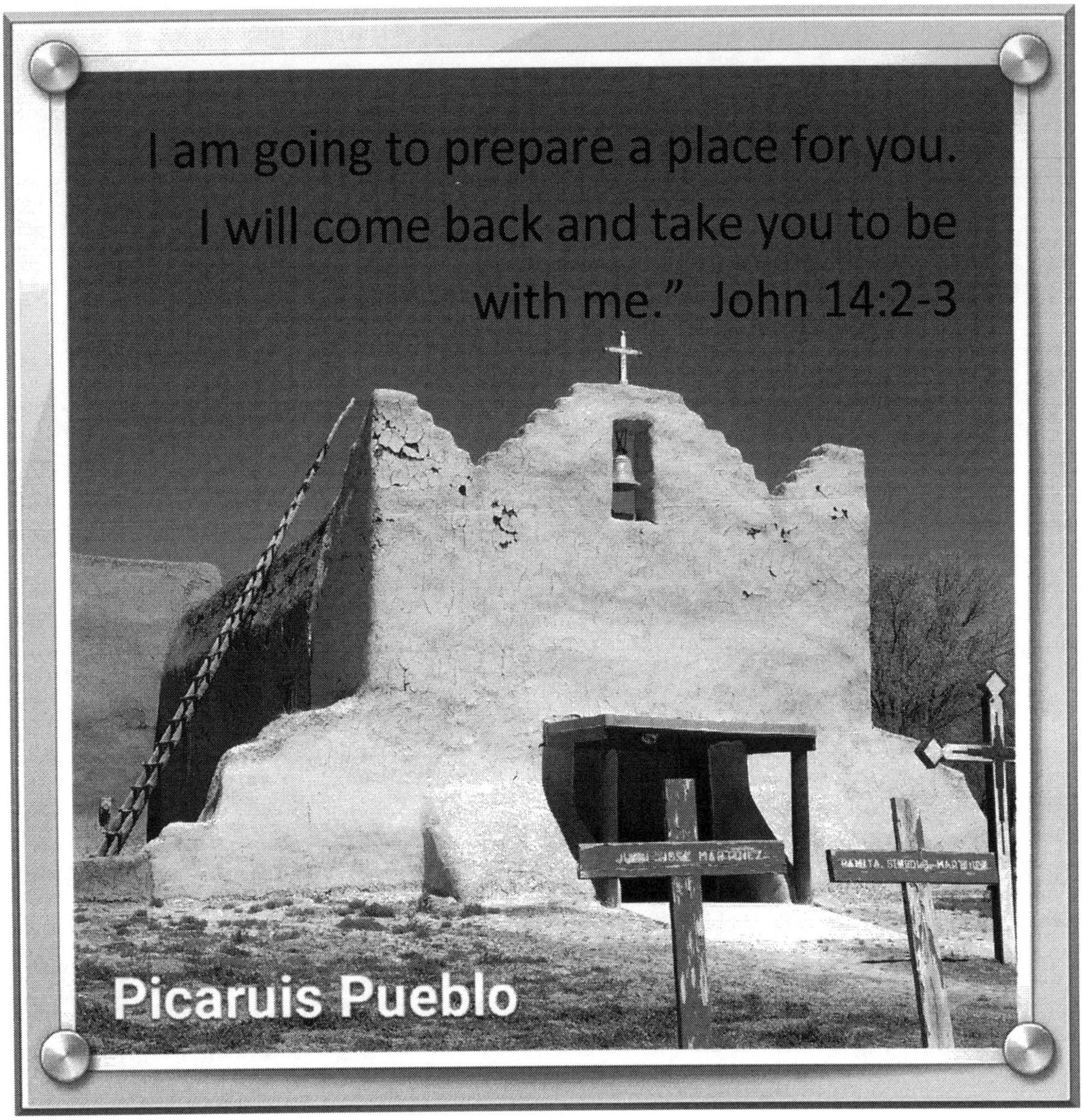
I am going to prepare a place for you.
I will come back and take you to be
with me." John 14:2-3
Picaruis Pueblo

UNIT 5 – HOUSING – LESSON 2 – HOME RENOVATIONS
STUDENT BOOK PAGE 97

A. Prayer for Students & Self

B. Lesson Objective and Functions:
- Describing common home renovations

C. Grammar Structures:
- Using WILL for Future

D. Biblical Reference or Principles:
- John 14:2

E. Materials & Preparation:
- For the Let's Practice Activity 3. Concentration, prepare a Concentration game board following directions in the Activity bank. Prepare Concentration card matches following directions under Let's Practice C. Conduct the Let's Practice Activity 3. Concentration.

<u>Introduction</u>

1. Ask: "What do you see in the picture?" [an old house before renovation and the same house renovated]
2. Ask: "Have you or anyone you know ever bought an old house and renovated it to make it new?"
3. Instructor tell any stories about home renovation projects you may have undertaken. If you cannot think of a story, feel free to use the following story about one of the author's students:
4. My student Barbara put a steak to cook on the stove one day then went outside to play basketball with her son. About 20 minutes later, her husband was driving home and shouting to her out the car window. The whole house was on fire! She forgot the steak and the kitchen caught fire. Fortunately, only the kitchen was burned. So, her husband renovated the kitchen and made it all brand new. It was beautiful. He was afraid to let her cook again in this new beautiful kitchen, so he made another kitchen outside in the yard and that was where Barbara had to do all her cooking! Her inside kitchen was just to look pretty.
5. Say: "Today we are going to learn vocabulary for some common home renovations."
6. Point out the vocabulary box, but don't teach it from this page.

UNIT 5

HOUSING

LESSON 2 – HOME RENOVATIONS

<u>Rooms</u>

bathroom

bedroom

kitchen

living room

<u>Fixtures</u>

granite countertops

Jacuzzi tub

stainless steel

appliances

vessel sink

<u>Features</u>

hardwood floors

wall-to-wall carpet

<u>Architectural Features</u>

crown molding

French doors

UNIT 5 – HOUSING – LESSON 2 – HOME RENOVATIONS
STUDENT BOOK PAGE 98

Introduce New Vocabulary

1. Have students open to Unit 5 – Housing; Lesson 2 – Home Renovations.
2. Introduce the words or phrases with a repetition drill. For instruction on conducting repetition drills, see Activity Bank. Repeat each 5-6 times.
3. Elicit conversation from students about the vocabulary by asking questions, such as:

- "What fixtures do you have in your bathroom? Shower? Jacuzzi tub? Vessel sink?"
- "What renovations would you like to make to your bathroom?"
- "What color is your bathroom tile? Walls? Floor?"

bathroom

vessel sink

jacuzzi tub

UNIT 5 – HOUSING – LESSON 2 – HOME RENOVATIONS
STUDENT BOOK PAGE 99

1. Continue introducing vocabulary of rooms, decorating features, and architectural features with a repetition drill.
2. Continue eliciting conversation about pictures, for example:
3. "Do you prefer carpet, wood, or tile floors? Why?"
4. "What kind of doors do you prefer: French doors with glass panels or solid doors?"

crown molding

French doors lead outside from the bedroom

wall-to-wall carpet in the bedroom

UNIT 5 – HOUSING – LESSON 2 – HOME RENOVATIONS
STUDENT BOOK PAGE 100

1. Continue introducing vocabulary of kitchen features with a repetition drill.
2. Continue eliciting conversation about pictures, for example:
    - "Do you prefer stainless steel appliances or something else?"
    - "What kind of counters do you have? Granite? Butcher block? Laminate?"
    - "Do you believe it is important to have granite counter tops? Why or why not?"

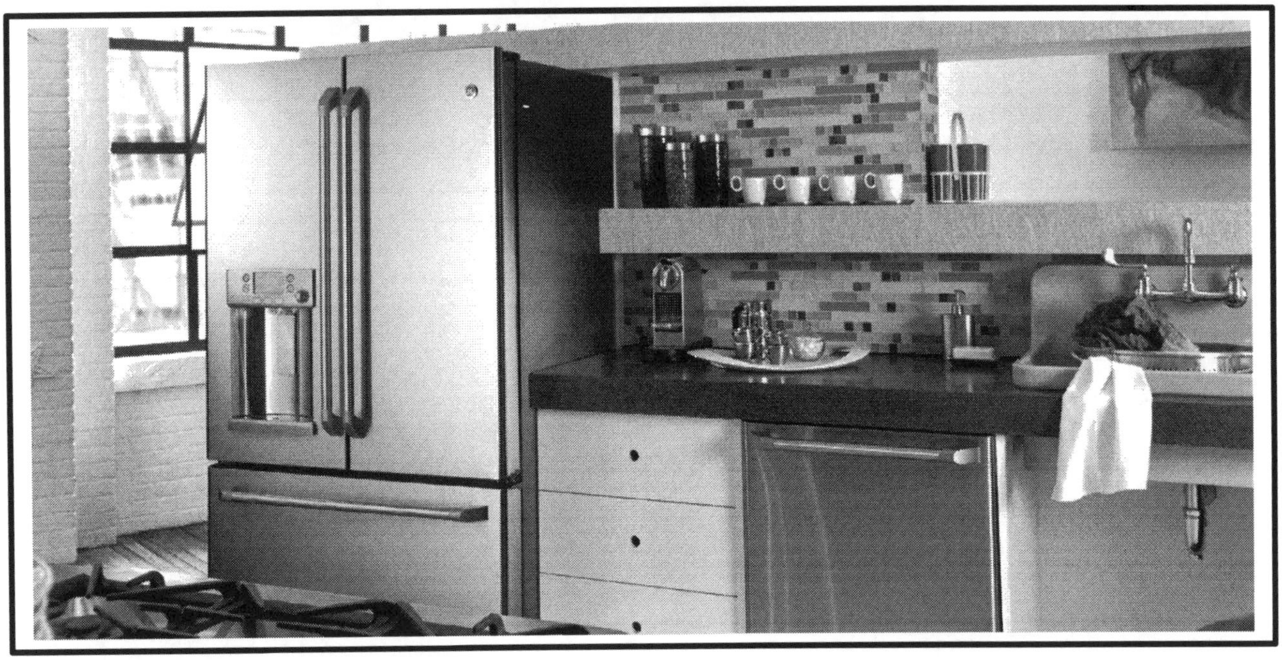

Top: granite countertops

Above: stainless steel appliances

UNIT 5 – HOUSING – LESSON 2 – HOME RENOVATIONS
STUDENT BOOK PAGE 101

Time to Speak

A. Conversation HOME RENOVATIONS

1. Ask: "Who are the 2 people in this conversation?"
2. Have students complete *To Do First* by having students repeat each line after the instructor. Repeat each line 5-6 times. Strive for a normal conversational tone rather than an oral reading tone.
3. Use backward build up for sentences longer than 4 words. Remember to divide sentences into sound units. See the Activity Bank for directions on backward build up and sound units.
4. Use correct intonation, stress, and rhythm patterns. Include the following intonation patterns:

- Statement (the voice starts higher and moves downward like going down a staircase through each sound unit in a statement. When the end of the statement is reached, at the period, the voice falls).
- WH-Question (The voice begins on a high note with the WH-Question word, then falls through the middle of the sentence until the last Content Word when the voice rises to accent the accented syllable in the last Content Word and then falls).
- AND/OR to Connect Two Items (voice goes up on the first item, down on AND, and then up and down on the second item.)

B. Have students complete *To Do Second* and *To Do Third*.
Call on individual student pairs to read the conversations after each Substitution has been drilled. Volunteer pairs present conversations for the class.

hardwood floors

To Do First: Repeat the conversation after the instructor.

To Do Second: Speak with a partner. Change the underlined words in the conversation for the Substitutions.

To Do Third: Change partners and repeat the Substitutions.

Time to Speak

Home Renovations

1.A. I'm renovating my **kitchen**.

1.B. Oh, how lucky for you. What changes are you making?

2.A. I'm getting **granite counter tops** and **stainless steel appliances**.

2.B. Well, good luck. I want to see your **kitchen** when you're finished.

3.A. Of course. I'll invite you to a party.

3.B. Sounds great.

Substitution No. 1

1.A. I'm renovating my **bathroom**.

1.B. Oh, how lucky for you. What changes are you making?

2.A. I'm getting **a Jacuzzi tub** and **a vessel sink**.

2.B. Well, good luck. I want to see your **bathroom** when you're finished.

3.A. Of course. I'll invite you to a party.

3.B. Sounds great.

UNIT 5 – HOUSING – LESSON 2 – HOME RENOVATIONS
STUDENT BOOK PAGE 102

Conclude Substitution Nos. 2 and 3.

Grammar Foundation

1. Complete *To Do First* by having students read the information under Future with WILL.
2. Have students complete *To Do Second* by having students repeat each example sentence after the instructor.
3. Ask for example sentences using the structures.
4. Repeat instructions to introduce Imperative Commands.

Substitution No. 2

1.A. I'm renovating my **bedroom**.

1.B. Oh, how lucky for you. What changes are you making?

2.A. I'm getting **wall-to-wall carpet** and **French doors** to the back yard.

2.B. Well, good luck. I want to see your **bedroom** when you're finished.

3.A. Of course. I'll invite you to a party.

3.B. Sounds great.

Substitution No. 3

1.A. I'm renovating my **living room**.

1.B. Oh, how lucky for you. What changes are you making?

2.A. I'm getting **hardwood floors** and **crown molding**.

2.B. Well, good luck. I want to see your **living room** when you're finished.

3.A. Of course. I'll invite you to a party.

3.B. Sounds great.

Grammar Foundation

Future with WILL

WILL is used with the simple form of the Verb to express future intention.

To Do First: Read the information about Future with WILL.

To Do Second: Repeat the example sentences after the instructor.

Statement

Subject + Will + Main Verb

I	will	invite	you to a party.
You	will	go	to the mall tomorrow.
He	will	call	the police.

.

UNIT 5 – HOUSING – LESSON 2 – HOME RENOVATIONS
STUDENT BOOK PAGE 103

Grammar Foundations Continued...

Continue introducing Contractions, Negatives, and Questions.

She	will	eat	ham and cheese
It	will	rain	tonight.
We	will	get	granite counter tops.
They	will	buy	wall-to-wall carpet.

The Subject is usually contracted with WILL

Contraction + Main Verb

I'll	see	your new kitchen next week.
You'll	love	the vessel sink after I put it in.
He'll	buy	stainless steel appliances on sale.
She'll	cook	pasta for the party.
We'll	have	French doors in our bedroom.
They'll	invite	me to a party next month.

Negative

Subject + Will + Not + Main Verb

I	will	not	buy crown molding.
You	will	not	get a Jacuzzi tub.
She	will	not	come to the party.
He	will	not	buy hardwood floors.
We	will	not	get granite counter tops.
They	will	not	finish the living room.

Subject + Contraction + Main Verb

I	won't	buy crown molding.
You	won't	get a Jacuzzi tub.
She	won't	come to the party.
He	won't	buy hardwood floors.
We	won't	get granite counter tops.
They	won't	finish the living room.

Question

Question Word + Will + Subject + Main Verb				Answer
	Will	you	buy a vessel sink?	Yes, I will.
	Will	she	put in stainless steel appliances?	No, she won't.
	Will	they	invite the builder to the party?	Yes, they will.
When	will	you	finish the renovation?	Next year.
What time	will	we	put in the crown molding?	After lunch.
Where	will	they	put the wall-to-wall carpet?	In the bedroom.

UNIT 5 – HOUSING – LESSON 2 – HOME RENOVATIONS
STUDENT BOOK PAGE 104

Correct the Mistakes

Each sentence has some mistakes.
Correct the mistakes.
Write the correct sentence on the line.

1. You go to the home improvement store tomorrow. ***You will go to the home improvement store tomorrow.***
2. He'll to buy grantie countertops. **He'll buy granite countertops.**
3. What time will you finishing the renovation? **What time will you finish the renovation?**
4. She will to get a vessel sink. **She will get a vessel sink.**
5. Will they won't get French doors. **They won't get French doors.**
6. You love the stainless steel appliances I will buy tomorrow. **You'll love the stainless steel appliances I will buy tomorrow.**
7. She'll will get a Jacuzzi tub and crown molding. **She will get a Jacuzzi tub and crown molding.**

Practicing Perfect Pronunciation

Two Items or Choices Connected with AND or OR

Demonstrate the Two Items Connected with AND or OR for the students. Both items are said with equal stress while the word that connects them, AND or OR, is said at a lower pitch. The first item goes up in pitch, and the second item goes up then down.

Have students repeat these items connected with AND from the conversations after the instructor:

1. granite counter tops and stainless steel appliances
2. a Jacuzzi tub and a vessel sink
3. wall-to-wall carpet and French doors
4. hardwood floors and crown molding

Correct the Mistakes

1. Each sentence has some mistakes.
2. Correct the mistakes.
3. Write the correct sentence on the line.

1. You go to the home improvement store tomorrow. ***You will go to the home improvement store tomorrow.***
2. He'll to buy granite countertops. ______________________
3. What time will you finishing the renovation? ______________________
4. She will to get a vessel sink. ______________________
5. Will they won't get French doors. ______________________
6. You love the stainless steel appliances I will buy tomorrow. ______________________
7. She'll will get a Jacuzzi tub and crown molding. ______________________

~~Practicing Perfect Pronunciation~~

Two Items or Choices Connected with AND or OR

Both items are said with equal stress while the word that connects them, AND or OR, is said at a lower pitch. The first item goes up in pitch, and the second item goes up then down.

Practice these items connected with AND from the conversations after the instructor:

1. granite counter tops and stainless steel appliances
2. a Jacuzzi tub and a vessel sink
3. wall-to-wall carpet and French doors
4. hardwood floors and crown molding

UNIT 5 – HOUSING – LESSON 2 – HOME RENOVATIONS
STUDENT BOOK PAGE 105

Let's Practice

A. Conduct the Let's Practice Activity 1. I Like/I Don't Like Dictation

1. Instructor dictates some home renovation products. If student would like to have the product, they should write it under the I LIKE column. If student would NOT like to have the product, write it under the I DON'T LIKE column.
2. Dictate the following 3-4 times each.

French doors	crown molding	granite countertops	vessel sink
Jacuzzi tub	stainless steel appliances		

B. Conduct the Let's Practice Activity 2. Survey

1. Students talk to their classmates.
2. Students ask which home renovations their classmates would like to do.
3. Students ask questions with WILL for Future, for example: "Will you buy a vessel sink?" Will you put in stainless steel appliances?"
4. Students should use any of the vocabulary including: crown molding, French doors, granite countertops, hardwood floors, Jacuzzi tub, stainless steel appliances, vessel sink, wall-to-wall carpet

Let's Practice

1. I Like/I Don't Like Dictation

1. The instructor will dictate some home renovation products.
2. If you would like to have the product, write it under the I LIKE column.
3. If you would NOT like to have the product, write it under the I DON'T LIKE column.

I LIKE	I DON'T LIKE
hardwood floors	
	wall-to-wall carpet
1.	
2.	
3.	
4.	
5.	
6.	

2. Survey

1. Talk to your classmates. Ask questions about home renovations they would like to do. Use WILL for Future, for example: "Will you buy a vessel sink? Will you put in stainless steel appliances?" Use any of the vocabulary including: crown molding, French doors, granite countertops, hardwood floors, Jacuzzi tub, stainless steel appliances, vessel sink, wall-to-wall carpet
2. Write the question you asked and their responses on your survey, for example: "Will you buy crown molding?"

Name	Questions: Will you buy . . .	Answers
Barbara	***crown molding***	***no***

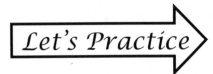

UNIT 5 – HOUSING – LESSON 2 – HOME RENOVATIONS
STUDENT BOOK PAGE 106

C. Conduct the Let's Practice Activity 3. Concentration

1. See Activity Bank for instructions on how to construct a Concentration game board and to prepare card matches.
2. For this activity, prepare in advance home renovation fixtures and feature card matches, including the following:

- crown molding
- Jacuzzi tub
- vessel sink
- French doors
- wall-to-wall carpet
- stainless steel appliances
- granite countertops

D. Conduct the Let's Practice Activity 4. Play Beat the Cat

1. For instructions on how to set up and play Beat the Cat, see Activity Bank.
2. Use this puzzle sentence: In my Father's house are many rooms.
3. NOTE: This is the Biblical principle. Instructor may wish to comment on the passage after puzzle is finished.
4. John 14:2: In my Father's house are many rooms. If it were not so, would I have told you that I go to prepare a place for you?

Review Exercises

Assign the Review Exercises for homework. Go over the instructions to ensure students understand how to complete each activity. **Answer Key in Bold**

1. What's the Next Line?

Read the statements. You will find two responses. Circle the correct response.

1. Will they invite the builder to the party?

A. Yes, they will. B. No, I don't want to go.

2. What color is your vessel sink?

A. I like vessel sinks. **B. It's green.**

____
____
____
____
____
____ 225

3. Concentration

1. Work with a partner or work with the whole class.
2. In the Concentration game board are some cards. Half of the cards have the first part of a fixture or feature, for example: 'Jacuzzi', and the other half of the cards have the second part of a fixture or feature, for example: 'tub.'
3. Student 1 chooses 2 cards from the Concentration board and reads them to the class. If the 2 cards match – they are removed from the board and Student 1 receives one point.
4. Student 2 chooses 2 cards from the Concentration board and reads them to the class. If the 2 cards do NOT match – Student 2 puts these cards back into the board.
5. Continue until all cards are matched and removed from the board.

4. Play Beat the Cat

1. This game is like the TV show Wheel of Fortune. The instructor will put a puzzle on the board.
2. Students take turns guessing consonants.
3. If the consonant is in the puzzle, the instructor will write it on the line. If the consonant is NOT in the puzzle, the instructor will draw part of a cat.
4. Continue until only vowels are left in the puzzle.

UNIT 5 – HOUSING – LESSON 2 – HOME RENOVATIONS
STUDENT BOOK PAGE 107

3. Will you buy wall-to-wall carpet for the bedroom?

A. No, just the living room. B. I'll buy crown molding.

4. James is renovating his bathroom.

A. Lucky for him. B. My husband is renovating my bedroom.

5. John bought French doors for his bedroom.

A. French doors will be nice. B. I will buy American doors.

Review Exercises

1. What's the Next Line?

Read the statements. You will find two responses. Circle the correct response.

1. Will they invite the builder to the party?

A. Yes, they will. B. No, I don't want to go.

2. What color is your vessel sink?

A. I like vessel sinks. B. It's green.

3. Will you buy wall-to-wall carpet for the bedroom?

A. No, just the living room. B. I'll buy crown molding.

4. James is renovating his bathroom.

A. Lucky for him. B. My husband is renovating my bedroom.

5. John bought French doors for his bedroom.

A. French doors will be nice. B. I will buy American doors.

2. My Dream House - Write a Paragraph

Write a paragraph of 6-8 sentences. Describe what your dream house looks like. You can answer these questions, for example:

1. How many bedrooms does it have?
2. How many bathrooms?
3. Where is this house?
4. Who lives in this house with you?
5. What kind of floors will your house have?
6. What kind of fixtures do you have in the bathroom?
7. What kind of appliances will you have in the kitchen?
8. Why do you like this house?

My dream house is in ____________________. It has ____________________

____

____

UNIT 5 – HOUSING – LESSON 2 – HOME RENOVATIONS
STUDENT BOOK PAGE 108

3. Mystery Word Search Puzzle

1. Complete the sentences below. For clues, see the Conversation and Substitutions What Did you Do Last Weekend?
2. Write the answers from the sentences on the lines in the puzzle. Put one letter on each line.
3. When finished, a mystery word will appear inside the box.
4. Write the mystery word on the line.

1. James will put in hardwood **floors** in his living room.
2. Joann will get new wall-to-wall **carpet** in her bedroom.
3. We will not get **stainless** steel appliances.
4. When will you finish putting in the **crown molding**?
5. Wow, that **Jacuzzi** tub is beautiful!
6. When will we renovate our **bathroom**?

```
1.                |f|l o o r s
2.            c a |r|p e t
3.  s t a i n l |e|s s
4.        c r o w |n|  m o l d i n g
5.            j a |c|u z z i
6.          b a t |h|r o o m
```

A mystery word will appear in the box. Write the mystery word here: **French.**

____

____

I like my dream house because ______________________________

____

3. Mystery Word Search Puzzle

1. Complete the sentences below. For clues, see the Conversation and Substitutions What Did you Do Last Weekend?
2. Write the answers from the sentences on the lines in the puzzle. Put one letter on each line.
3. When finished, a mystery word will appear inside the box.
4. Write the mystery word on the line.

1. James will put in hardwood ______________ in his living room.
2. Joann will get new wall-to-wall ____________ in her bedroom.
3. We will not get __________________ steel appliances.
4. When will you finish putting in the __________ _______________?
5. Wow, that _________________ tub is beautiful!
6. When will we renovate our ___________________?

```
1.                 |_|_ _ _ _ _
2.             _ _ |_|_ _ _
3.   _ _ _ _ _ _ _ |_|_ _
4.       _ _ _ _ _ |_| _ _ _ _ _ _ _
5.             _ _ |_|_ _ _ _
6.           _ _ _ |_|_ _ _ _
```

A mystery word will appear in the box. Write the mystery word here: ______________.

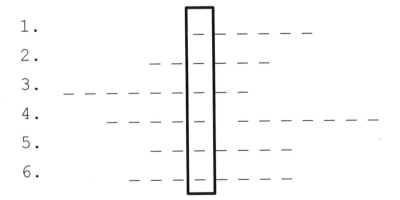

UNIT 5 – HOUSING – LESSON 3 – HOME REPAIRS
STUDENT BOOK PAGE 109

A. Prayer for Students & Self

B. Lesson Objective and Functions:
- Describing home repair attempts and calling a repair person

C. Grammar Structures:
- Questions with DO and BE

D. Biblical Reference or Principles:
- The Wise and Foolish Builders Matthew 7:24-27: Everyone who hears my words and puts them into practice is like a wise man who built his house on the rock. The rain came down, the flood waters came up, and the wind blew against the house; but the house did not fall down because it was built on the rock. But everyone who hears my words and does not put them into practice is like the foolish man who built his house on the sand. The rain came down, the flood waters came up, and the wind blew against the house, and the house fell down with a great crash.

E. Materials & Preparation:
- For the Let's Practice Activity 1. Concentration, prepare 3x5 Concentration game card matches. See the Let's Practice Activity 1. for the matches.

<u>Introduction</u>

1. Instructor describes a home repair you've had to make. If you cannot think of any, then you may use the following story from the author: "Our toilet was broken, so my husband went to Home Depot and bought a new toilet. He came home and took out the broken toilet. Then he put in the new toilet. When he was finished, I came in to see the new toilet. It wasn't white. It was bone colored. My husband looked at the box. The box said "white" but the toilet was bone colored. So, my husband had to take out the new toilet, return it to Home Depot, and get a white toilet. At home he had to put in the new white toilet. It was a lot of work! Next time, I think we'll call a plumber to do the work."

2. Ask: "Who has a story about a house repair that you'd like to tell?" [get student response]

3. Say: " Today, we are going to talk about different kinds of repair problems in our houses and how we can get the repair done."

4. Point out the vocabulary box, but don't teach it from this page.

UNIT 5
HOUSING

LESSON 3 – HOME REPAIRS

Condition	Repair Actions	Repair Persons	Nouns
broken	fix – fixing	electrician	oven element
burned out	plunge - plunging	plumber	plunger
clogged	repair – repairing		sink
doesn't get hot	replace – replacing		stove burner

UNIT 5 – HOUSING – LESSON 3 – HOME REPAIRS
STUDENT BOOK PAGE 110

Introduce New Vocabulary

1. Have students open to Unit 5 – Housing; Lesson 3 – Home Repairs.
2. Introduce the words or phrases with a repetition drill. For instruction on conducting repetition drills, see Activity Bank. Repeat each 5-6 times.
3. Elicit conversation from students about the vocabulary by asking questions, such as:
4. "Have you ever had a broken appliance? An oven, a stove, refrigerator, dish washer, washing machine, dryer? Did you repair it yourself? Did you call a repair service? Did you buy a new appliance? Tell about your experiences."

Previous page: an electrician repairing a broken oven

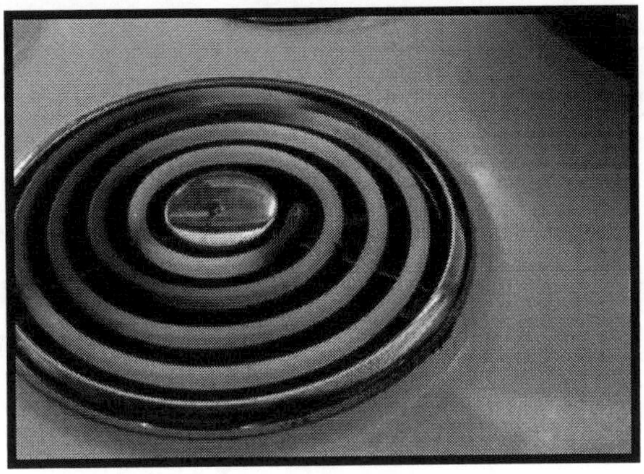

electric stove coil doesn't get hot

electric stove top

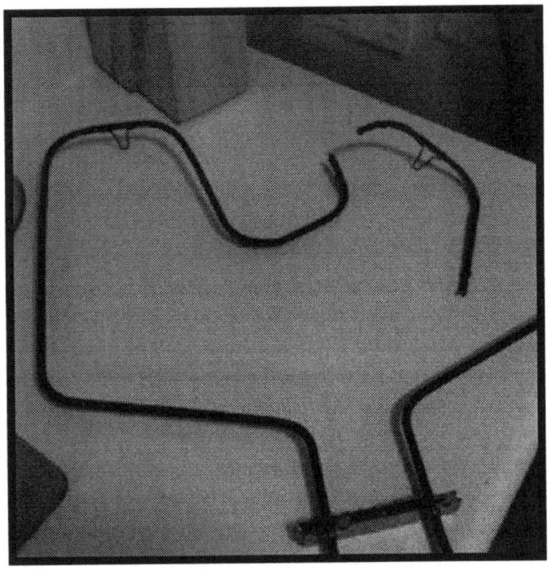

broken oven element

replacing an oven element

UNIT 5 – HOUSING – LESSON 3 – HOME REPAIRS
STUDENT BOOK PAGE 111

1. Continue introducing vocabulary words and phrases with a repetition drill.
2. Continue eliciting conversation about pictures.

clogged kitchen sink

plunging the clogged sink

plumber
fixing
kitchen
sink

UNIT 5 – HOUSING – LESSON 3 – HOME REPAIRS
STUDENT BOOK PAGE 112

Time to Speak

A. Conversation Repairs and Maintenance

1. Ask: "Who are the 2 people in this conversation?"
2. Have students complete *To Do First* by having students repeat each line after the instructor. Repeat each line 5-6 times. Strive for a normal conversational tone rather than an oral reading tone.
3. Use backward build up for sentences longer than 4 words. Remember to divide sentences into sound units. See the Activity Bank for directions on backward build up and sound units.
4. Use correct intonation, stress, and rhythm patterns. Include the following intonation patterns:

- Statement (the voice starts higher and moves downward like going down a staircase through each sound unit in a statement. When the end of the statement is reached, at the period, the voice falls).
- WH-Question (The voice begins on a high note with the WH-Question word, then falls through the middle of the sentence until the last Content Word when the voice rises to accent the accented syllable in the last Content Word and then falls).
- YES/NO Question (The voice rises at the end of each Sound Unit and rises dramatically at the end of the sentence).

B. Have students complete *To Do Second* and *To Do Third*.
Call on individual student pairs to read the conversations after each Substitution has been drilled. Volunteer pairs present conversations for the class.

C. Have students complete *To Do Fourth* by changing partners and using the conversation and substitutions as a model to create their own conversations. Volunteers present their conversations for the class.

Time to Speak

Repairs and Maintenance

Speaker A: Repair person

Speaker B: Home owner

1.A. **Eddie's Electrical**. May I help you?

1.B. Yes. My **oven and stove don't get hot**.

2.A. **Are the elements burned out**?

2.B. **The stove burner comes on half way.**

3.A. O.K. We can send **an electrician** out at **3:30 p.m**.

3.A. O.K.

4.A. What's your name and address?

4.B. My name is **Keeley Davies**. My address is **14801 Archer Hall Street, Davie**.

Substitution No. 1

1.A. **Phil's Plumbing**. May I help you?

1.B. Yes. My **sink is clogged**.

2.A. **Did you try a plunger**?

2.B. **Yes, but it's still clogged.**

3.A. O.K. We can send **a plumber** out at **10:00 a.m**.

3.B. O.K.

4.A. What's your name and address?

4.B. My name is **James Murphy**. My address is **8900 S.W. 51 Court, Cooper City**.

To Do First: Repeat the conversation after the instructor.

To Do Second: Speak with a partner. Change the underlined words in the conversation for the Substitutions.

To Do Third: Change partners and repeat the Substitutions.

To Do Fourth: Change partners. Use the conversation to talk about yourselves.

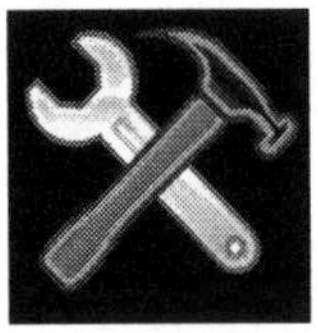

UNIT 5 – HOUSING – LESSON 3 – HOME REPAIRS
STUDENT BOOK PAGE 113

Grammar Foundation

1. Complete *To Do First* by having students read the information under Asking Questions with DO, DOES or DID.
2. Have students complete *To Do Second* by having students repeat each example sentence after the instructor.

Grammar Foundation

To Do First: Read the information about Asking Questions with DO, DOES or DID.

Asking Questions with DO, DOES or DID

1. Use the auxiliary verb DO for action verbs
2. Use DOES for third person.
3. Use DID for the Past Tense

Do/Does	+ Subject	+ Main Verb		Short Answers
Do	I	know	you?	No, I don't. (do not)
Do	you	unclog	sinks?	Yes, I do.
Do	we	live	in America?	Yes, we do.
Do	they	use	the oven?	No, they don't.
Does	he	repair	ovens?	No, he doesn't. (does not)
Does	she	work	at Phil's Plumbing?	Yes, she does.
Does	it	snow	in Miami?	No, it doesn't.

To Do Second: Repeat example sentences after the instructor.

Question Word	+ Did	+ Subject	+ Main Verb		Answers
	Did	you	change	the burner?	Yes, I did.
	Did	John	fix	the sink?	No, he didn't.
	Did	he	try	a plunger?	Yes, he did.
	Did	they	fix	the stove?	No, they didn't.
What	did	you	do	yesterday?	I fixed my stove.
When	did	John	change	the bulbs?	He changed the bulbs yesterday.
When	did	the element burn out?			It burned out today.
Why	did	they	call	a plumber?	Because their sink was clogged.

UNIT 5 – HOUSING – LESSON 3 – HOME REPAIRS
STUDENT BOOK PAGE 114

Grammar Foundation Continued...

1. Complete *To Do First* by having students read the information under Asking Questions with BE.
2. Have students complete *To Do Second* by having students repeat each example sentence after the instructor.

Asking Questions with the BE Verb

1. When the main verb is BE we do not use the auxiliary verb DO.
2. We use the BE verb at the beginning of the structure.
3. The Be Verb is used to describe a State of Being. We use it to describe how we are or who we are, or a place we are at. See examples below.

To Do First: Read the information about Asking Questions with BE.

To Do Second: Repeat example sentences after the instructor.

Be + Subject			Short Answers	Contraction Form
Are	you	a student?	Yes, I am.	(None)
Is	he	at home?	No, he is not.	No, he isn't. -or- No, he's not.
Is	the oven	burned out?	No, it is not.	No, it isn't. -or- No, it's not.
Is	your sink	clogged?	Yes, it is.	(none)
Are	we	plumbers?	Yes, we are.	(none)
Are	they	at home?	No, they are not.	No, they aren't. -or- No, they're not.

More examples of BE:

How We Are:	Who We Are:	Where We Are:
Are you happy? Yes, I am.	Are you a student? Yes.	Are you at church? Yes, I am.
Is she hungry? No, she isn't.	Is she a mother? No.	Is she at work? Yes, she is.
Is he well? Yes, he is.	Is he an uncle? Yes, he is.	Is he at church? No, he's not.
Are we tired? Yes, we are.	Are we friends? Yes, we are.	Are we in Macy's? No, we're not.
Are they absent? Yes.	Are they sisters? No.	Are they in New York? Yes.

UNIT 5 – HOUSING – LESSON 3 – HOME REPAIRS
STUDENT BOOK PAGE 115

Grammar Foundation Continued...

1. Begin the exercises Asking Do and Be Questions by going over the examples.
2. Complete Nos. 1.-4. together as a class.
3. Ensure students understand how to formulate both the question and the short answer using the sentence in parentheses.
4. Assign Nos. 5.-8. for homework.

Practicing Perfect Pronunciation

Have students repeat these tongue twisters after the instructor. They are practicing some sounds from the conversation and substitutions.

1. Paul the plumber plunged the pretty pukey clog with the plunger.
2. Elaine the electrician elected to eliminate the old electric element.

Asking Do and Be Questions

1. Make questions and give short answers.
2. Use the information in the parentheses to make the questions and answers.

Examples: A: ***Did you plunge the clogged sink?***

B: ***Yes, I did.*** (I plunged the sink.)

A: ***Are you an electrician?***

B. ***Yes, I am.*** (I am an electrician.)

1. A: ______________________________________

   B: ____________________ (Their sink is clogged.)

2. A: ______________________________________

   B: ____________________ (He goes to church at St. James.)

3. A: ______________________________________

   B: ____________________ (We're not cooking on the stove tonight.)

4. A: ______________________________________

   B: ____________________ (He replaced the oven element.)

5. A: ______________________________________

   B: ____________________ (My parents are from Russia.)

6. A: ______________________________________

   B: ____________________ (He uses the stove every day.)

7. A: ______________________________________

   B: ____________________ (The stove isn't working today.)

8. A: ______________________________________

   B: ____________________ (The electrician repairs ovens and stoves.)

~~Practicing Perfect Pronunciation~~

Practice these tongue twisters with sounds from the conversation. Repeat each after the instructor.

1. Paul the plumber plunged the pretty pukey clog with the plunger.
2. Elaine the electrician elected to eliminate the old electric element.

UNIT 5 – HOUSING – LESSON 3 – HOME REPAIRS
STUDENT BOOK PAGE 116

Let's Practice

A. Conduct the Let's Practice Activity 1. Concentration

For instructions on how to construct a Concentration game board and how to play Concentration, see Activity Bank.

Prepare 3x5 Concentration card matches:

1. The plunger didn't unclog my sink.	Call a plumber.
2. My sink is clogged.	Try a plunger.
3. My stove doesn't get hot.	Call an electrician.
4. My oven doesn't get hot.	Call an electrician.
5. My oven element is broken.	Replace the element.

B. Conduct the Let's Practice Activity 2. Call a Repair Person/Do It Myself – Dictation

1. Have students open to the Let's Practice Activity 2. Call a Repair Person/Do It Myself – Dictation activity.
2. Instructor will dictate some home repair conditions.
3. Tell the students that if the condition is one for which they would call a repair person, write it under the Call a Repair Person column.
4. If the condition is one for which they would NOT call a repair person, write it under the Do It Myself column.
5. When finished, go over student responses.

Dictate the following, repeating each one 3-4 times:

1. my kitchen light doesn't turn on
2. my toilet doesn't flush
3. there's a rat in my house
4. my bath tub is clogged
5. my oven element is burned out

Let's Practice

1. Concentration

1. Work with a partner or work with the whole class.
2. In the Concentration game board are some cards. Half of the cards have home repair conditions and the other half of the cards have repair person. For example: clogged sink = plumber.
3. Student 1 chooses 2 cards from the Concentration board and reads them to the class. If the 2 cards match – they are removed from the board and Student 1 receives one point.
4. Student 2 chooses 2 cards from the Concentration board and reads them to the class. If the 2 cards do NOT match – Student 2 puts these cards back into the board.
5. Continue until all cards are matched and removed from the board.

2. Call a Repair Person/Do It Myself - Dictation

1. The instructor will dictate some home repair conditions.
2. If the condition is one for which you would call a repair person, write it under the Call a Repair Person column.
3. If the condition is one for which you would NOT call a repair person, write it under the Do It Myself column.

Call a Repair Person	Do It Myself
My stove doesn't get hot.	
	My sink is clogged.
1.	
2.	
3.	
4.	
5.	

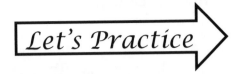

UNIT 5 – HOUSING – LESSON 3 – HOME REPAIRS
STUDENT BOOK PAGE 117

C. Conduct the Let's Practice Activity 3. My House Repair Experience – Pair, Square, Share

For information on conducting a Pair, Square, Share, see the Activity Bank.
For this activity, students are sharing a home repair experience.

D. Conduct the Let's Practice Activity 4. Cloze Listening Passage

1. Read the passage at a normal rate of speed. Remind students this is a real world listening activity so you will not stop during the reading, but you will read as many times as they request. It is not uncommon for students to request 4 or more readings.
2. Students write the missing words on the lines. **Teacher Answer Key and Transcript in Bold.** There are 13 missing words.
3. When finished, ask for volunteers to read sections aloud to check student responses.

NOTE: This is the Biblical principle. Instructor may wish to comment on the passage when finished.

The Wise and Foolish Builders Matthew 7:24-27

Everyone who ***hears*** my words and puts them **into** practice is like a wise man who built his **house** on the rock. The rain came down, the flood **waters** came up, and the **wind** blew against the **house**; but the house did not fall **down** because it was built on the rock. **But** everyone who hears my words and does not put **them** into practice is like the foolish **man** who built his house on the **sand**. The rain came down, the flood waters came up, and the wind blew against the **house**, and the **house** fell down with a **great** crash.

3. My House Repair Experience – Pair, Square, Share

1. Work with a partner. Student 1 tells about a house repair he/she had to make.
2. Student 2 summarizes Student 1's story.
3. Student 2 tells about a house repair he/she had to make.
4. Student 1 summarizes Student 2's story.
5. When finished, listen for the instructor's directions.

4. Cloze Listening Passage

1. Listen to the instructor read the passage.
2. Write the missing words on the lines.
3. The instructor will read as often as students request.

The Wise and Foolish Builders

Matthew 7:24-27

Everyone who ***hears*** ________ my words and puts them __________ practice is like a wise man who built his ________________ on the rock. The rain came down, the flood ________________ came up, and the ________________ blew against the ____________; but the house did not fall __________________ because it was built on the rock. _________ everyone who hears my words and does not put ____________ into practice is like the foolish ________________ who built his house on the ______________. The rain came down, the flood waters came up, and the wind blew against the ______________, and the _________ fell down with a __________________ crash.

UNIT 5 – HOUSING – LESSON 3 – HOME REPAIRS
STUDENT BOOK PAGE 118

Review Exercises

Assign the Review Exercises for homework. Go over the instructions to ensure students understand how to complete each activity. **Answer Key in Bold**

1. Complete the Conversation

Read the conversation. Circle the correct word in the [brackets].

Adel's Home Repair Troubles

By Barbara K. Black

Adel is unhappy today. He wanted to cook breakfast for his wife. He wanted to make eggs. The [**stove** / sink] wouldn't get hot. So, he called Eddie's [Plumbing / **Electrical**]. Eddie asked, "Is the electric [**stove** / oven] coil burned out?" Adel looked at the [oven / **stove**] coil. "It's half burned out," Adel replied. Eddie asked, "[Does / **Do**] you want me to come repair it?" Adel said, "No, I [do / **don't**]. I will use the oven instead." So, Adel decided he would make some banana bread for breakfast. Adel mixed the banana bread. He put it into a pan. Then, Adel put it into the [**oven** / stove]. After one hour he looked at the banana bread. Oh, no! The oven didn't get [cold / **hot**]. The banana bread [was / **was not**] baked. Adel looked at the oven [coil / **element**]. It was broken. Adel called Eddie's Electrical again. "My oven element is [**broken** / broke]," said Adel. "Do you want me to come [look / **replace**] it?" asked Eddie. Adel said, "No, I [do / **don't**] . I will use the microwave." So Adel used the microwave to bake the banana bread. Then Adel looked in the newspaper. He saw that Appliance Depot had a sale on ovens and [sinks / **stoves**]. He went to Appliance Depot and bought a new oven and [sink / **stove**]. Adel was very happy. He called Eddie's Electrical. "Will you come and install my new [**oven** / sink] and stove?" Adel asked. Eddie said, "Yes, I [won't / **will**]."

2. Hidden Word Puzzle

Circle the words in the puzzle.

BURNED OUT	ELEMENT	BURNER	STOVE	OVEN	ELECTRICIAN
SINK	CLOGGED	PLUNGER	PLUMBER	REPAIR	REPLACE

N K H K E W O J E S A T U S N K L Q I U W E O P Y U B V C X P A
S D F G H K L N M B S D F G ***P L U M B E R*** S A P Q I D N I U Y T
R E W Q K L K ***E L E M E N T*** J H H G F D S S A W N T O N M B V C
X D E N I O N W T Q J T H E M N I O P W N J G N ***O V E N*** K L N I
E T N E L N D G N X T C X T T R M N N I O P Y T N B G F M I V Y

Review Exercises

1. Complete the Conversation

Read the conversation. Circle the correct word in the [brackets].

Adel's Home Repair Troubles

By Barbara K. Black

Adel is unhappy today. He wanted to cook breakfast for his wife. He wanted to make eggs. The [stove / sink] wouldn't get hot. So, he called Eddie's [Plumbing / Electrical]. Eddie asked, "Is the electric [stove / oven] coil burned out?" Adel looked at the [oven / stove] coil. "It's half burned out," Adel replied. Eddie asked, "[Does / Do] you want me to come repair it?" Adel said, "No, I [do / don't]. I will use the oven instead." So, Adel decided he would make some banana bread for breakfast. Adel mixed the banana bread. He put it into a pan. Then, Adel put it into the [oven / stove]. After one hour he looked at the banana bread. Oh, no! The oven didn't get [cold / hot]. The banana bread [was / was not] baked. Adel looked at the oven [coil / element]. It was broken. Adel called Eddie's Electrical again. "My oven element is [broken / broke]," said Adel. "Do you want me to come [look / replace] it?" asked Eddie. Adel said, "No, I [do / don't] . I will use the microwave." So Adel used the microwave to bake the banana bread. Then Adel looked in the newspaper. He saw that Appliance Depot had a sale on ovens and [sinks / stoves]. He went to Appliance Depot and bought a new oven and [sink / stove]. Adel was very happy. He called Eddie's Electrical. "Will you come and install my new [oven / sink] and stove?" Adel asked. Eddie said, "Yes, I [won't / will]."

2. Hidden Word Puzzle

Circle the words in the puzzle.

BURNED OUT	ELEMENT	BURNER	STOVE	OVEN	ELECTRICIAN
SINK	CLOGGED	PLUNGER	PLUMBER	REPAIR	REPLACE

```
N K H K E W O J E S A T U S N K L Q I U W E O P Y U B V C X P A
S D F G H K L N M B S D F G P L U M B E R S A P Q I D N I U Y T
R E W Q K L K E L E M E N T J H H G F D S S A W N T O N M B V C
X D E N I O N W T Q J T H E M N I O P W N J N O V E N K L N I N
E T N E L N D G N X T C X T T R M N N I O P Y T N B G F M I V Y
```

UNIT 5 – HOUSING – LESSON 3 – HOME REPAIRS
STUDENT BOOK PAGE 119

B U R N E R F A G E W Q U Y T R N B J A S M J F A T U N H E R N

K O Q **R E P A I R** W N K T N A N K N I Q W N **B U R N E D O U T** E

I B T E W Q I Y W I C X S I N Q W E R R B N V C Q N I Y T R E Q

N **S T O V E** I O N W T A L O H W A N Y S N I Y I O W T N Q I O U

Y T H N K **R E P L A C E** A T N N I U Y E N M L W O N T E W Q N V

J A L N Q W E R T Y I O P N K **P L U N G E R** H H A Z I S W T I Y

N I W T R W O R K N N T N N I I O Y Y I I N I E T G D A B N I N

E N B X O N Q W E R T **E L E C T R I C I A N** F R D E W B N I N O

I N O T E N I W O T O A S V T N I N K H I Y E N S T T H I M E S

Q W E R T Y U I O B M T T T N I N D A L S Y N I Y R T W Q N M B

X B V W T N I S E T D W T I Y **S I N K** O W E N A I Y I O P T A N

D D I X X V B C N I Q T Y G A I X S S G T O T E X B Q B N J S B

D A C B N K G N W Z T A B E N I T O K O A M N S G N K H G B D A

C L O G G E D K W I N G O N A B C E G H T G F D S A N K O Y A Q

E N T P I C N G I N A M I Y N B E T Q T N I O W O R C O K I N G

Barbara Kinney Black

B U R N E R F A G E W Q U Y T R N B J A S M J F A T U N H E R N

K O Q R E P A I R W N K T N A N K N I Q W N B U R N E D O U T E

I B T E W Q I Y W I C X S I N Q W E R R B N V C Q N I Y T R E Q

N S T O V E I O N W T A L O H W A N Y S N I Y I O W T N Q I O U

Y T H N K R E P L A C E A T N N I U Y E N M L W O N T E W Q N V

J A L N Q W E R T Y I O P N K P L U N G E R H H A Z I S W T I Y

N I W T R W O R K N N T N N I I O Y Y I I N I E T G D A B N I N

E N B X O N Q W E R T E L E C T R I C I A N F R D E W B N I N O

I N O T E N I W O T O A S V T N I N K H I Y E N S T T H I M E S

Q W E R T Y U I O B M T T T N I N D A L S Y N I Y R T W Q N M B

X B V W T N I S E T D W T I Y S I N K O W E N A I Y I O P T A N

D D I X X V B C N I Q T Y G A I X S S G T O T E X B Q B N J S B

D A C B N K G N W Z T A B E N I T O K O A M N S G N K H G B D A

C L O G G E D K W I N G O N A B C E G H T G F D S A N K O Y A Q

E N T P I C N G I N A M I Y N B E T Q T N I O W O R C O K I N G

UNIT 6 – MEDICAL – LESSON 1 – HEALTHY LIVING
STUDENT BOOK PAGE 120

A. Prayer for Students & Self

B. Lesson Objective and Functions:
   - Undersanding doctor's advice for healthy behavioral changes

C. Grammar Structures:
   - Using SHOULD to give advice

D. Biblical Reference or Principles:
   - Ezekiel 37:1-14 - Ezekiel's vision of the dry bones.

Introduction

1. Say: "Today we are going to talk about changes in our lives to become more healthy. What are some kinds of changes you would like to make or someone you know wants to make?" [Write student responses on board. Give an example first such as lose weight.]
2. Choose one of the responses such as lose weight.
3. Ask: "What steps do you recommend to take if someone wants to lose weight?"
4. Write student responses on board.
5. Point out the vocabulary box, but don't teach it from this page.

UNIT 6
MEDICAL

LESSON 1 – HEALTHY LIVING

Doctor's Orders	Doctor's Advice	
lose weight	call a friend	join a support group
stop drinking alcohol	do some activity	use the patch
stop smoking	eat a low carb diet	
	eat chicken and fish, fruits and vegetables	

UNIT 6 – MEDICAL – LESSON 1 – HEALTHY LIVING
STUDENT BOOK PAGE 121

Introduce New Vocabulary

1. Have students open to Unit 6 – Medical; Lesson 1 – Healthy Living.
2. Introduce the words or phrases with a repetition drill. For instruction on conducting repetition drills, see Activity Bank. Repeat each 5-6 times.

3. Elicit conversation from students about the vocabulary by asking questions, such as:

- "What do you do when you want to lose weight?"
- "Do you like chicken and fish?"
- "What kinds of fruits and vegetables do you like to eat?"
- "Have you ever been on a low carb diet?"

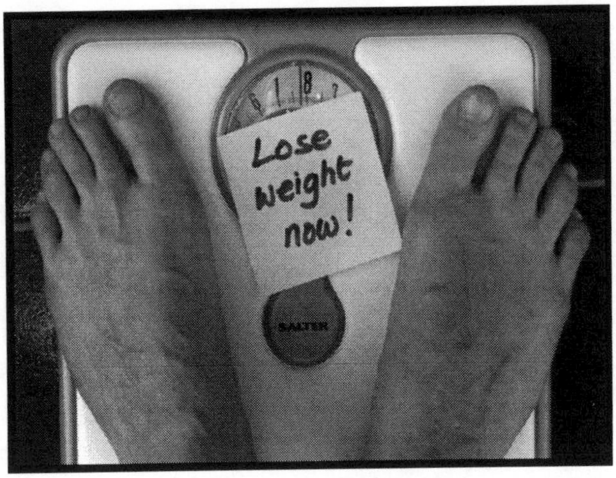

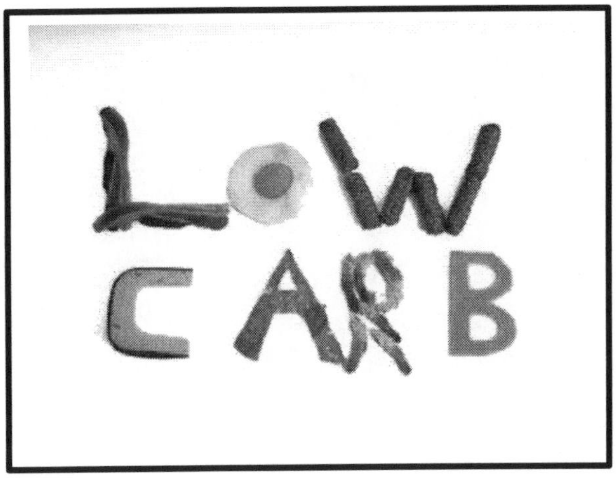

lose weight

eat a low carb diet

Eat chicken and fish,
fruits and vegetables

UNIT 6 – MEDICAL – LESSON 1 – HEALTHY LIVING
STUDENT BOOK PAGE 122

1. Continue introducing vocabulary words and phrases with a repetition drill.
2. Continue eliciting conversation about pictures.

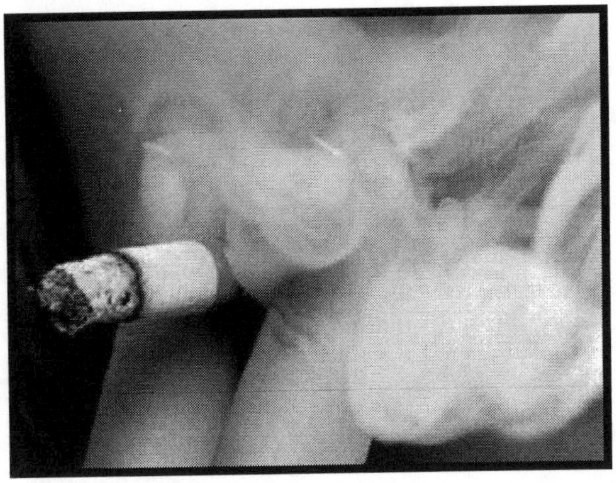

stop smoking

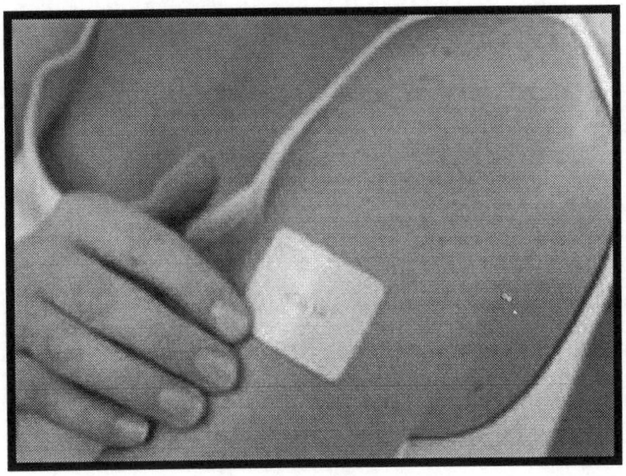

use the patch

stop drinking alcohol

join a support group

UNIT 6 – MEDICAL – LESSON 1 – HEALTHY LIVING
STUDENT BOOK PAGE 123

Time to Speak

A. Conversation Healthy Living

1. Ask: "Who are the 2 people in this conversation?"
2. Have students complete *To Do First* by having students repeat each line after the instructor. Repeat each line 5-6 times. Strive for a normal conversational tone rather than an oral reading tone.
3. Use backward build up for sentences longer than 4 words. Remember to divide sentences into sound units. See the Activity Bank for directions on backward build up and sound units.
4. Use correct intonation, stress, and rhythm patterns. Include the following intonation patterns:

- Statement (the voice starts higher and moves downward like going down a staircase through each sound unit in a statement. When the end of the statement is reached, at the period, the voice falls).
- WH-Question (The voice begins on a high note with the WH-Question word, then falls through the middle of the sentence until the last Content Word when the voice rises to accent the accented syllable in the last Content Word and then falls).

B. Have students complete *To Do Second* and *To Do Third*.
Call on individual student pairs to read the conversations after each Substitution has been drilled. Volunteer pairs present conversations for the class.

C. Have students complete *To Do Fourth* by changing partners and using the conversation and substitutions as a model to create their own conversations. Volunteers present their conversations for the class.

Time to Speak

Healthy Living

Speaker A: Doctor

Speaker B: Patient

> *To Do First:* Repeat the conversation after the instructor.
>
> *To Do Second:* Speak with a partner. Change the underlined words in the conversation for the Substitutions.
>
> *To Do Third:* Change partners and repeat the Substitutions.

1.A. Your physical examination shows you are mostly in good health.

    1.B. That's good.

2.A. Still, I think you should **lose 20 pounds**.

    2.B. I 've tried to **lose weight**, but it's difficult.

3.A. You should eat **a low carb diet.**

    3.B. **What should I eat**?

4.A. You should eat **chicken and fish, fruits and vegetables**.

    4.B. O.K. Thanks.

Substitution No. 1

1.A. Your physical examination shows you are mostly in good health.

    1.B. That's good.

2.A. Still, I think you should **stop smoking**.

    2.B. I've tried to **stop smoking**, but it's difficult.

3.A. You should **use the stop smoking patch**.

    3.B. What should I do when **I want a cigarette**?

4.A. You should **do some activity**.

    4.B. O.K. Thanks.

UNIT 6 – MEDICAL – LESSON 1 – HEALTHY LIVING
STUDENT BOOK PAGE 124

Grammar Foundation

1. Complete *To Do First* by having students read the information under Using SHOULD to Give Advice.
2. Have students complete *To Do Second* by having students repeat each example sentence after the instructor.

Substitution No. 2

1.A. Your physical examination shows you are mostly in good health.

1.B. That's good.

2.A. Still, I think you should **stop drinking alcohol**.

2.B. I've tried to **stop drinking alcohol**, but it's difficult.

3.A. You should **join a support group**.

3.B. What should I do when **I want a drink**?

4.A. You should **call a friend**.

4.B. O.K. Thanks.

Grammar Foundation

Using SHOULD or SHOULDN'T to Give Advice or Make Suggestions

We use SHOULD to give advice or make suggestions. Here's the structure:

Affirmative

Subject + SHOULD + Main Form of Verb

I	should	drink	more water.
You	should	study	English.
He	should	lose	weight.
She	should	eat	her vegetables.
We	should	stop	drinking alcohol.
They	should	do	exercise every day.

To Do First: Read the information about Using SHOULD or SHOULDN'T to Give Advice or Make Suggestions.

To Do Second: Repeat example sentences after the instructor.

Negative

Subject + SHOULD + Not + Main Form of Verb

I	shouldn't	eat	candy.
You	shouldn't	smoke.	
He	shouldn't	drink	too much alcohol.

UNIT 6 – MEDICAL – LESSON 1 – HEALTHY LIVING
STUDENT BOOK PAGE 125

Grammar Foundation Continued…

- Lead students in completing Nos. 1.-4. in the Correct the Mistakes activity. Assign Nos. 5.-7. for homework.

She	shouldn't	eat	a high carb diet.
We	shouldn't	read	this book.
They	shouldn't	watch	too much T.V.

Questions

Question +	SHOULD +	Subject +	Main Form of Verb		Short Answers
	Should	I	eat	a low carb diet?	Yes, you should.
	Should	you	eat	at McDonalds?	No, I shouldn't.
	Should	Marie	stop	smoking?	Yes, she should.
	Should	he	drink	alcohol every day?	No, he shouldn't.
What	should	I	do	tonight?	Study English.
How	should	he	lose	weight?	Go on a low carb diet.
Why	should	she	drink	milk?	Because milk is good for her.
Where	should	we	go	this summer?	To Colombia.
What time	should	they	visit	us tonight?	At 7:30 p.m.

Correct the Mistakes

1. Each sentence has some mistakes.
2. Correct the mistakes.
3. Write the correct sentence on the line.

1. The doctor said I should not to lose 20 lbs. ***The doctor said I should lose 20 lbs.***
2. He should stop smoke. ____________________
3. They should to do exercise every day. ____________________
4. What should do to lose weight? ____________________
5. Should join a support group to stop smoking. ____________________
6. I to should eat lots of candy. ____________________
7. What should Henry do when to want a drink? ____________________

UNIT 6 – MEDICAL – LESSON 1 – HEALTHY LIVING
STUDENT BOOK PAGE 126

Let's Practice

A. Conduct the Let's Practice Activity 1. Doctor and Patient Conversations Listening Activity

1. Listen to the Doctor/Patient conversations.
2. Write the missing words on the lines.

Conversation 1

1. Your ***physical examination*** shows you are mostly in good health.
2. That's **great**.
3. Still, I think you **should** exercise 3-5 days a week.
4. Exercise? Why should I **exercise**?
5. You have high blood pressure. The **exercise** will help to bring down the blood pressure.
6. What kind of exercise **should** I do?
7. **I think** you should go for a walk.

Conversation 2

1. Your **physical** examination shows you are mostly in good health.
2. Excellent.
3. Still, I think **you should** eat less salt and fat.
4. **Eat** less salt and **fat?** Why?
5. You need to **lose weight**. If you eat less salt and fat you'll lose weight.
6. What can I **eat?**
7. I think **you should** eat fish and **chicken**, fruits and **vegetables,** and eat less starches.

Conversation 3

1. Your physical examination shows you are in bad health.

Let's Practice

1. Doctor and Patient Conversations Listening Activity

1. Listen to the Doctor/Patient conversations.
2. Write the missing words on the lines.

Conversation 1

1. Your ***physical examination*** shows you are mostly in good health.
2. That's ____________________.
3. Still, I think you _________________ exercise 3-5 days a week.
4. Exercise? Why should I _____________________?
5. You have high blood pressure. The ________________ will help to bring down the blood pressure.
6. What kind of exercise ________________ I do?
7. ____________________ you should go for a walk.

Conversation 2

1. Your ____________________ examination shows you are mostly in good health.
2. Excellent.
3. Still, I think ____________________ eat less salt and fat.
4. _________ less salt and ___________? Why?
5. You need to _________________________. If you eat less salt and fat you'll lose weight.
6. What can I __________?
7. I think ________________________ eat fish and ________________, fruits and ____________________________, and eat less starches.

Conversation 3

1. Your physical examination shows you are in bad health.

UNIT 6 – MEDICAL – LESSON 1 – HEALTHY LIVING
STUDENT BOOK PAGE 127

2. Oh, no!
3. I think you should stop **smoking** and **drinking** alcohol.
4. Why should I stop smoking and drinking?
5. **You should** stop smoking and drinking or you will be dead in one year.
6. O.K. **I think** I should stop **smoking** and drinking alcohol.
7. That's a good idea!

B. Conduct the Let's Practice Activity 2. Play Beat the Cat
For instructions on how to set up and play Beat the Cat, see Activity Bank. Use this puzzle sentence: "You should use the stop smoking patch to stop smoking."

C. Conduct the Let's Practice Activity 3. Them Bones
NOTE: This is the Biblical principle. Instructor may wish to comment on the passage which is taken from Ezekiel 37:1-14 Ezekiel's vision of the dry bones.

1. This is a song. If you are unfamiliar with how the song sounds, try finding it on the Internet. It is a traditional spiritual song. Note that there are many versions of the song on the Internet – not all have retained the traditional wording. If you don't know the song and can't find it online, then perhaps just chant the song.
2. Teach the words of the song with a repetition drill. Note the [rest] in the Chorus which syncopates the rhythm.
3. Lead students in the song. Have students touch the body part as they sing.

2. Oh, no!
3. I think you should stop _______________ and __________________ alcohol.
4. Why ___________________________stop smoking and drinking?
5. _________________________ stop smoking and drinking or you will be dead in one year.
6. O.K. _____________________ I should stop _____________________ and drinking alcohol.
7. That's a good idea!

2. Play Beat the Cat

1. This game is like the TV show Wheel of Fortune. The instructor will put a puzzle on the board.
2. Students take turns guessing consonants.
3. If the consonant is in the puzzle, the instructor will write it on the line. If the consonant is NOT in the puzzle, the instructor will draw part of a cat.
4. Continue until only vowels are left in the puzzle.

3. Them Bones

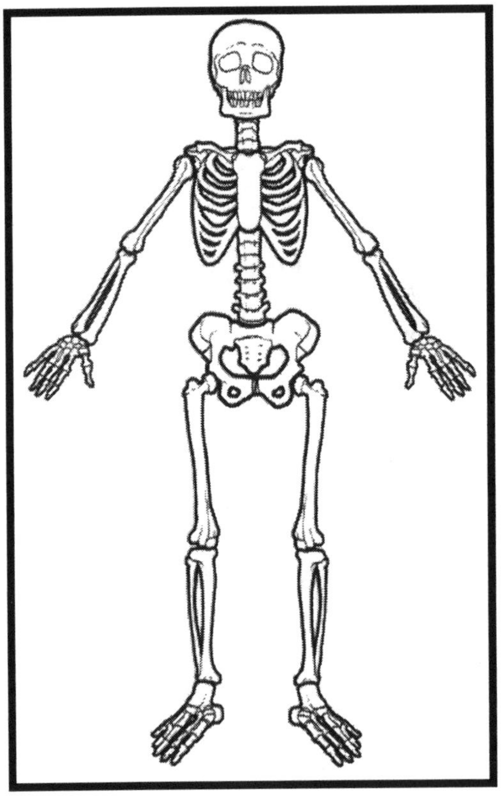

This is a song. The instructor will teach students the song.

As students sing the song, they should touch the body part as they sing it. For example, when you sing, "The toe bone's connected to the foot bone," touch first your toe, then touch your foot.

Chorus

Them bones, them bones, them, [rest] dry bones
Them bones, them bones, them, [rest] dry bones.
Them bones, them bones, them, [rest] dry bones.
Now hear the Word of the Lord.

UNIT 6 – MEDICAL – LESSON 1 – HEALTHY LIVING
STUDENT BOOK PAGE 128

Review Exercises

Assign the Review Exercises for homework. Go over the instructions to ensure students understand how to complete each activity. **Answer Key in Bold**

1 Scrambled Sentence

1. The doctor said / I should / join a / support group / to help / me lose / weight.
2. I think / we should / go on a / low carb / diet.
3. Would you / like to eat / chicken / or fish / tonight?
4. What kind / of fruits / and vegetables / do you / like to cook?
5. My doctor / said I should / stop / drinking / alcohol all the / time.
6. Would you / buy a / stop smoking / patch / for me when / you are at / the supermarket / today?

Verse 1

The toe bone's connected to the [rest] foot bone.

The foot bone's connected to the [rest] leg bone.

The leg bone's connected to the [rest] hip bone,

Now hear the Word of the Lord. Repeat CHORUS

Verse 2

The hip bone's connected to the [rest] back bone.

The back bone's connected to the [rest] neck bone.

The neck bone's connected to the [rest] head bone,

Now hear the Word of the Lord. Repeat CHORUS

This song talks about a story in the Scripture from Ezekiel 37:1-14 - Ezekiel's vision of the dry bones.

Review Exercises

1. Scrambled Sentence

Put the words of the sentences into correct order. Use all the words.

1. I should / join a / to help / The doctor said / me lose / support group / weight.
2. we should / diet / go on a / I think / low carb.
3. or fish / Would you / chicken / tonight? / like to eat
4. of fruits / What kind / do you / like to cook? / and vegetables
5. alcohol all the / said I should / stop / My doctor /drinking / time.
6. buy a / stop smoking / for me when / Would you / you are at / the supermarket / patch / today?

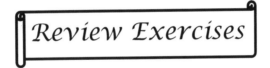

UNIT 6 – MEDICAL – LESSON 1 – HEALTHY LIVING
STUDENT BOOK PAGE 129

2. Mystery Word Search Puzzle

1. Complete the sentences below. For clues, see the Conversation and Substitutions What Did you Do Last Weekend?
2. Write the answers from the sentences on the lines in the puzzle. Put one letter on each line.
3. When finished, a mystery word will appear inside the box.
4. Write the mystery word on the line.

Part 1:

1. The doctor said I should lose 20 **pounds**.
2. When I want a cigarette I should **do some activity**.
3. What do you think about a **low carb** diet?

1. I love to eat **chicken**.
2. I need to eat more healthy **fish**.
3. The doctor said I should **join a group** to help me stop drinking alcohol.
4. Use the patch to stop smoking **cigarettes.**

```
1.   P O U N D|S|
2.   D O   S O|M|E   A C T I V I T Y
3.           L|O|W   C A R B
4.     C H I C|K|E N
5.           F|I|S H
6.       J O I|N|  A   G R O U P
7.         C I|G|A R E T T E S
```

A mystery word will appear in the box. Write it on the line: **smoking.**

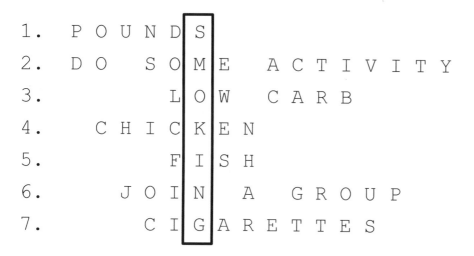

2. Mystery Word Search Puzzle

1. Complete the sentences below. For clues, see the Conversation and Substitutions What Did you Do Last Weekend?
2. Write the answers from the sentences on the lines in the puzzle. Put one letter on each line.
3. When finished, a mystery word will appear inside the box.
4. Write the mystery word on the line.

1. The doctor said I should lose 20 ____________.
2. When I want a cigarette I should ______ ________ _________________.
3. What do you think about a __________ ____________ diet?
4. I love to eat _________________.
5. I need to eat more healthy ______________.
6. The doctor said I should ________ _____ ____________ to help me stop drinking alcohol.
7. Use the patch to stop smoking _____________________.

```
1.  _ _ _ _ _|_|
2.  _ _   _ _|_|_   _ _ _ _ _ _ _ _
3.          _|_|_   _ _ _ _
4.    _ _ _ _|_|_ _
5.          _|_|_ _
6.      _ _ _|_|  _   _ _ _ _ _
7.        _ _|_|_ _ _ _ _ _ _
```

A mystery word will appear in the box. Write it on the line: ______________.

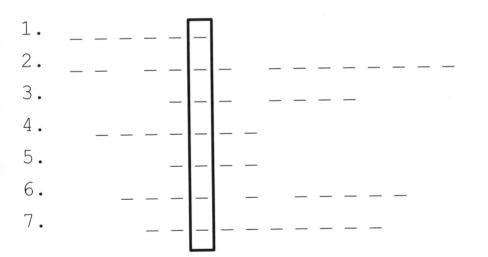

UNIT 6 – MEDICAL – LESSON 2 – STAYING WELL
STUDENT BOOK PAGE 130

A. Prayer for Students & Self

B. Lesson Objective and Functions:
- Describing medical symptoms and illness preventative measures

C. Grammar Structures:
- Using AND to Connect Two Ideas that are Similar

D. Biblical Reference or Principles:
- Mark 2:17 – Jesus heard this and said to them, "Healthy people don't need a doctor. It is the sick who need a doctor. I did not come to invite good people. I came to invite sinners."

E. Materials & Preparation:
- For the Let's Practice Activity 2. Ball Toss – koosh ball or other soft object to toss. Alternately, use a wadded up piece of paper to make a ball.

<u>Introduction</u>

1. Have students look at the picture on the first page of the lesson. Read the inscription, "Be Healthy! Eat well, Live well."
2. Ask: "What do you think about this inscription? What role does what we eat play in our health?"
3. Ask: "What foods do you consider to be healthy foods? What foods do you consider to be not healthy? Why?"
4. Ask: "Do you think you can take actions to help stay well? What kinds of actions could you take to stay well?
5. "Say: "Today we will talk about the ways people try to stay well."
6. Point out the vocabulary box, but don't teach it from this page.

UNIT 6
MEDICAL

LESSON 2 – STAYING WELL

Illness	Preventative Actions		
a cold	drink hot tea with lemon & honey	stay home & rest	wear a
the flu	immune defense supplement	take Vitamin C	mask
a store throat	stay away from sick people	wash your hands	flu shot

UNIT 6 – MEDICAL – LESSON 2 – STAYING WELL
STUDENT BOOK PAGE 131

Introduce New Vocabulary

1. Have students open to Unit 6 – Medical; Lesson 2 – Staying Well.
2. Introduce the words or phrases with a repetition drill. For instruction on conducting repetition drills, see Activity Bank. Repeat each 5-6 times.
3. Elicit conversation from students about the vocabulary by asking questions, such as:

- "What do you do when you think you are getting the flu?"
- "Do you take Vitamin C? What other vitamins do you take to stay well?"

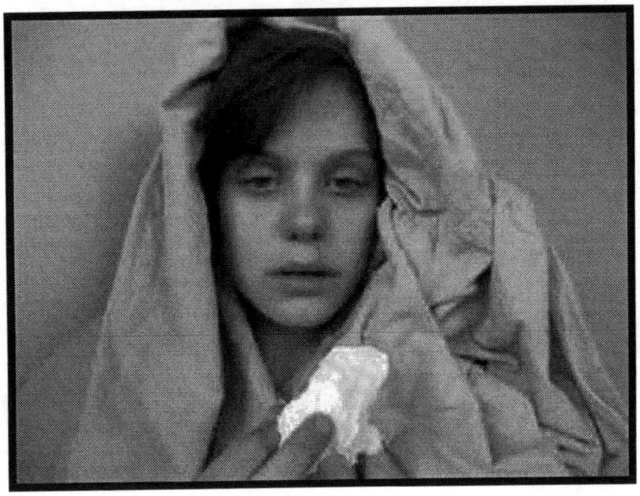

getting the flu

take Vitamin C

stay away from sick people

UNIT 6 – MEDICAL – LESSON 2 – STAYING WELL
STUDENT BOOK PAGE 132

Continue introducing vocabulary words and phrases with a repetition drill. Continue eliciting conversation by asking questions related to the words.

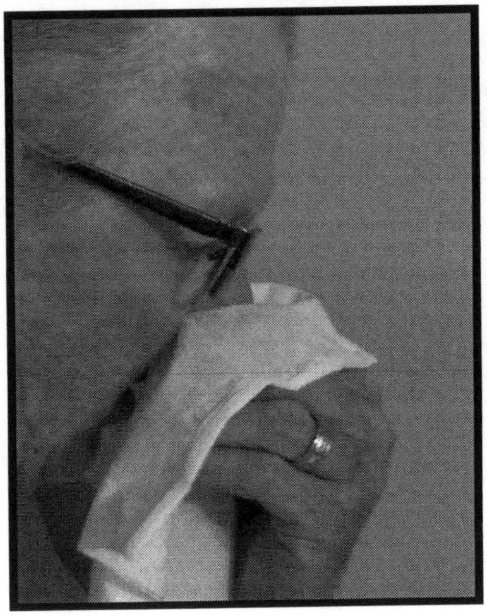

have a cold

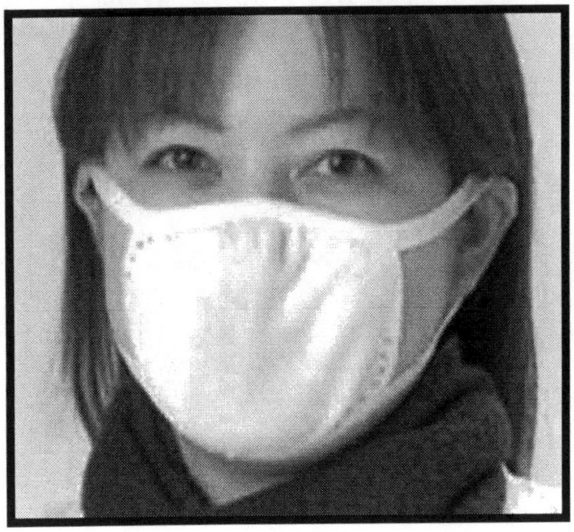

wear a mask

wash my hands a lot

UNIT 6 – MEDICAL – LESSON 2 – STAYING WELL
STUDENT BOOK PAGE 133

1. Continue introducing vocabulary words and phrases with a repetition drill.
2. Continue eliciting conversation by asking questions related to the words.
3. Read the question in the box.
4. Instructor answers question about him/herself.
5. Direct students to talk to a partner and share their tips for staying well.

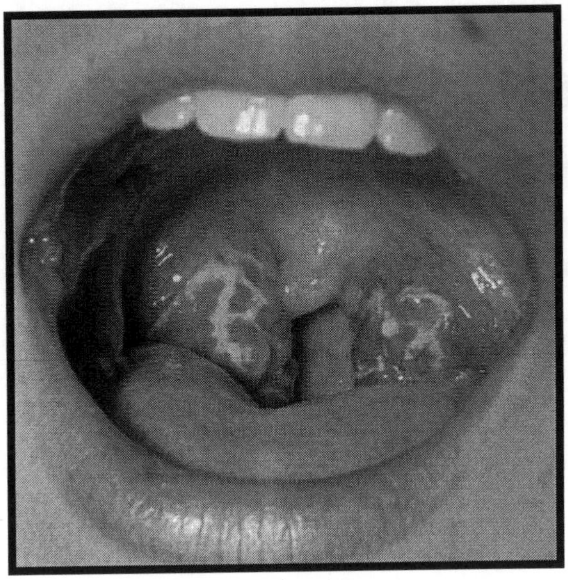

I have a sore throat

drink hot tea with lemon and honey

How do you stay well?
Talk to a partner.

take
throat
lozenges

UNIT 6 – MEDICAL – LESSON 2 – STAYING WELL
STUDENT BOOK PAGE 134

Time to Speak

A. Conversation Staying Well

1. Ask: "Who are the 2 people in this conversation?"
2. Have students complete *To Do First* by having students repeat each line after the instructor. Repeat each line 5-6 times. Strive for a normal conversational tone rather than an oral reading tone.
3. Use backward build up for sentences longer than 4 words. Remember to divide sentences into sound units. See the Activity Bank for directions on backward build up and sound units.
4. Use correct intonation, stress, and rhythm patterns. Include the following intonation patterns:

- Statement (the voice starts higher and moves downward like going down a staircase through each sound unit in a statement. When the end of the statement is reached, at the period, the voice falls).
- WH-Question (The voice begins on a high note with the WH-Question word, then falls through the middle of the sentence until the last Content Word when the voice rises to accent the accented syllable in the last Content Word and then falls).

B. Have students complete *To Do Second* and *To Do Third*.
Call on individual student pairs to read the conversations after each Substitution has been drilled. Volunteer pairs present conversations for the class.

Time to Speak

Staying Well

1.A. I'm **getting the flu**.

1.B. So, how are you planning to stay well?

2.A. I'll **take Vitamin C** and **stay away from sick people**.

2.B. Those are good ideas.

To Do First: Repeat the conversation after the instructor.

To Do Second: Speak with a partner. Change the underlined words in the conversation for the Substitutions.

To Do Third: Change partners. Use the conversation to talk about yourselves.

Substitution No. 1

1.A. I'm **catching a cold**.

1.B. So, how are you planning to stay well?

2.A. I'll **wear a mask** and **wash my hands a lot**.

2.B. Those are good ideas.

Substitution No. 2

1.A. I'm **getting a sore throat**.

1.B. So, how are you planning to stay well?

2.A. I'll **drink hot tea with lemon and honey** and **take throat lozenges**.

2.B. Those are good ideas.

UNIT 6 – MEDICAL – LESSON 2 – STAYING WELL
STUDENT BOOK PAGE 135

Grammar Foundation

1. Complete *To Do First* by having students read the information under Using AND to Connect Two Ideas that are Similar.
2. Have students complete *To Do Second* by having students repeat each example sentence after the instructor.

Practicing Perfect Pronunciation

Practice the AND/OR Intonation Pattern. See Activity Bank for more information. Have students repeat lines 2.A. from the conversation and Substitutions.

Using AND to Connect Two Ideas that are Similar

We use the Conjunction AND to connect two ideas in the same sentence. For example:

First Idea +	AND +	Second Idea
I am going to stay home	and	eat a healthy dinner.
John has a cold	and	a headache.
We are studying Speech	and	Grammar.
Noah built an ark	and	saved the animals.
I'll wear a mask	and	wash my hands a lot.

Finish the sentences with the ideas in the box.

1. I'm going to take throat lozenges ______________________
2. John is going to take some cold medicine ______________________
3. Mary is wearing a mask ______________________
4. Is Tom sick? He is washing his hands a lot ______________________
5. I am taking Vitamin C ______________________

a. and washing her hands a lot.

b. and go to bed early.

c. and drink hot tea.

d. and wearing a mask.

e. and throat lozenges.

~~Practicing Perfect Pronunciation~~

Using the AND/OR Intonation Pattern

Both items are said with equal stress while the word that connects them, AND or OR, is said at a lower pitch. For the first item, raise the voice at the end of the item. For the second item, the voice goes up then down on the end.

Practice the AND/OR Intonation Pattern by repeating lines 2.A. from the conversation Staying Well and the Substitutions 1. and 2. After the instructor.

UNIT 6 – MEDICAL – LESSON 2 – STAYING WELL
STUDENT BOOK PAGE 136

Let's Practice

A. Conduct the Let's Practice Activity 1. I Like/I Don't Like Dictation

1. Instructor dictate illness preventative measures.
2. Students write the preventative measure under the column I LIKE if it is a measure they like to take.
3. Students write the measure under the column I DON'T LIKE if it is a measure they don't wish to take.
4. Go over student responses when finished.

Include these preventative measures:

1. Drink hot tea with lemon & honey
2. Take an immune defense supplement
3. Stay away from sick people
4. Stay home & rest
5. Wash your hands

B. Conduct the Let's Practice Activity 2. Ball Toss

1. Use a koosh ball or wadded up piece of paper as a ball or other soft object to toss.
2. The instructor names an illness and tosses a ball to Student 1.
3. Student 1 names the illness preventative measure and tosses the ball back to the instructor.
4. For example: The instructor says, "cold." Student 1 catches the ball and says, "wear a mask."
5. Continue until all have participated multiple times.

Let's Practice

1. I Like/I Don't Like Dictation

1. The instructor will dictate some illness preventative measures.
2. If you would like to take this preventative measure, write it under the I LIKE column.
3. If you would NOT like to take this preventative measure, write it under the I DON'T LIKE column.

I LIKE	I DON'T LIKE
taking Vitamin C	
	wearing a mask

1. ____________________
2. ____________________
3. ____________________
4. ____________________
5. ____________________
6. ____________________
7. ____________________

2. Ball Toss

1. The instructor will name an illness and toss a ball to Student 1.
2. Student 1 names the illness preventative measure and tosses the ball back to the instructor.
3. For example: The instructor says, "cold." Student 1 catches the ball and says, "wear a mask."

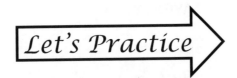

UNIT 6 – MEDICAL – LESSON 2 – STAYING WELL
STUDENT BOOK PAGE 137

C. Conduct the Let's Practice Activity 3. Survey

1. Students talk to each other asking questions about their illness preventive actions.
2. Students write their interviewee's responses on their surveys.
3. When finished, go over student responses with the class.

D. Conduct the Let's Practice Activity 4. Scrambled Spelling

1. Have students work with a small group.
2. Read the paragraph below.
3. Students unscramble the spelling of the underlined words. Write the correct word on the line.
4. Students read their paragraph to the class.
5. When finished, the instructor may wish to comment on the passage.

Teacher Answer Key and Transcript in Bold

Mark 2:17 – Jesus [**heard** a d e h r ______] this and said to them, " [**Healthy** a e h h l t y ____________] people don't need a [**doctor** c d o o r t ___] . It is the [**sick** c i k s ___] who need a doctor. I did not [**come** c e m o ____________] to invite good people. I came to [**invite** e i i n t v] sinners."

3. Survey

1. Talk to your classmates. Ask questions about their illness preventative actions, for example: "What do you do when you are getting the flu?"
2. Write their responses on your survey, for example: "Carmen takes Vitamin C."

Name	What do you do when you are getting the flu?	What do you do when you are getting a sore throat?
1.		
2.		
3.		
4.		

4. Scrambled Spelling

1. Work with a small group.
2. Read the paragraph below.
3. Unscramble the spelling of the underlined words. Write the correct word on the line.
4. Read your paragraph to the class.

Mark 2:17 – Jesus [a d e h r ______________] this and said to them,
"[a e h h l t y ______________] people don't need a [c d o o r t ______________].
It is the [c i k s ______________] who need a doctor. I did not
[c e m o ______________] to invite good people. I came to
[e i i n t v ______________] sinners."

UNIT 6 – MEDICAL – LESSON 2 – STAYING WELL
STUDENT BOOK PAGE 138

Review Exercises

Assign the Review Exercises for homework. Go over the instructions to ensure students understand how to complete each activity. **Answer Key in Bold**

1. Reading Comprehension True or False

1. Read the paragraph.
2. Read the statements about the paragraph.
3. Circle True or False.

Teacher Answer Key in Bold

Chicken Soup Conquers a Cold

By Barbara K. Black

When you have a cold, you might eat chicken soup. Many people believe chicken soup will help them get well again.
So, how does chicken soup help get rid of a cold?

1. True **False** Everyone believes chicken soup helps you get well again.

First, chicken soup loosens the mucus secretions in your nose. Then hot chicken soup makes your nose run. When your nose runs, you get rid of bacteria from the body. Chicken soup gives the body lots of fluids to keep you hydrated. Finally, chicken soup warms up your airways so you can breathe easier.

2. **True** False Chicken soup loosens mucus secretions.
3. **True** False Chicken soup makes your nose run.
4. True **False** Chicken soup doesn't keep you hydrated.
5. **True** False Chicken soup helps you breathe easier.

Chicken soup usually has chicken, chicken broth, and vegetables, for example: onions, sweet potatoes, parsnips, turnips, carrots, celery stems, and parsley. Some chicken soups have noodles or rice. Of course, all chicken soup has salt and pepper.

6. **True** False Chicken soup has chicken broth.
7. **True** False Chicken soup has 7 kinds of vegetables.
8. True **False** Chicken soup always has noodles and rice.

So, the next time you have a cold, get rid of it fast – eat chicken soup.

Review Exercises

1. Reading Comprehension True or False

1. Read the paragraph.
2. Read the statements about the paragraph.
3. Circle True or False.

Chicken Soup Conquers a Cold

By Barbara K. Black

When you have a cold, you might eat chicken soup. Many people believe chicken soup will help them get well again.

So, how does chicken soup help get rid of a cold?

1. True False Everyone believes chicken soup helps you get well again.

First, chicken soup loosens the mucus secretions in your nose. Then hot chicken soup makes your nose run. When your nose runs, you get rid of bacteria from the body. Chicken soup gives the body lots of fluids to keep you hydrated. Finally, chicken soup warms up your airways so you can breathe easier.

2. True False Chicken soup loosens mucus secretions.
3. True False Chicken soup makes your nose run.
4. True False Chicken soup doesn't keep you hydrated.
5. True False Chicken soup helps you breathe easier.

Chicken soup usually has chicken, chicken broth, and vegetables, for example: onions, sweet potatoes, parsnips, turnips, carrots, celery stems, and parsley. Some chicken soups have noodles or rice. Of course, all chicken soup has salt and pepper.

6. True False Chicken soup has chicken broth.
7. True False Chicken soup has 7 kinds of vegetables.
8. True False Chicken soup always has noodles and rice.

So, the next time you have a cold, get rid of it fast – eat chicken soup.

UNIT 6 – MEDICAL – LESSON 2 – STAYING WELL
STUDENT BOOK PAGE 139

2. Hidden Word Puzzle

Circle the words in the puzzle.

FLU	COLD	SORE THROAT	IMMUNE DEFENSE
WASH	VITAMIN C	WEAR A MASK	GET A FLU SHOT

N K H K E W O J E S A T U S N K L Q I U W E O P Y U B V C X P A

S D F G H K L N M B S D F G S A P ***S O R E T H R O A T*** Q I D N I

U Y T R E W Q K L K J H H G F D S S A W N T O N M B V C X D E N

I O N W T Q J T H E M N I O P W N J ***W A S H*** N K L N I N E T N E

L N D G N X T C X T T R M N N I O P Y T N B G F M I V Y F A G E

W Q U Y T R N B J A S M J F A T U N H E ***F L U*** R N K O Q W N K T

N A N K E W Q O U B R N I Q W N E I B T E W Q I Y W I C X S I N

Q W E R R B N V C Q N I Y T R E Q ***C O L D*** N I O N W T A L O H W

A N Y S N I Y I O W T N Q I O U Y T H N K A T N N I U Y E N M L

W O N T E W Q N V J A L N Q W E R T Y I O P N K H G E N H H A Z

I S W T I Y N I W T R W O R ***I M M U N E D E F E N S E*** I I N I E

T G D A B N I N E N B X O N Q W E R T F R D E W B N F D S R W N

I N O I ***G E T A F L U S H O T*** N O T E N I W O T O A S V T N I N

K H I Y E N S T T H I M E S Q W E R T Y U I O B M T T T N I N D

A L S Y N I Y R T W Q N M B X B V W T N I S E T D W T I Y O W E

N A I Y I O P T A N D D I X X V B C N I Q T Y G A N J K E O Q N

U E R I X S S ***V I T A M I N C*** G T O T E X B Q B N J S B D A C B

N K G N W Z T A B E N I T O K O A M N S G N K H G B D A K W I N

G O N A B C E G H T G F ***W E A R A M A S K*** D S A N K O Y A Q E N

T P I C N G I N A M I Y N B E T Q T N I O W O R C O K I N G N I

2. Hidden Word Puzzle

Circle the words in the puzzle.

FLU	COLD	SORE THROAT	IMMUNE DEFENSE
WASH	VITAMIN C	WEAR A MASK	GET A FLU SHOT

```
N K H K E W O J E S A T U S N K L Q I U W E O P Y U B V C X P A
S D F G H K L N M B S D F G S A P S O R E T H R O A T Q I D N I
U Y T R E W Q K L K J H H G F D S S A W N T O N M B V C X D E N
I O N W T Q J T H E M N I O P W N J W A S H N K L N I N E T N E
L N D G N X T C X T T R M N N I O P Y T N B G F M I V Y F A G E
W Q U Y T R N B J A S M J F A T U N H E F L U R N K O Q W N K T
N A N K E W Q O U B R N I Q W N E I B T E W Q I Y W I C X S I N
Q W E R R B N V C Q N I Y T R E Q C O L D N I O N W T A L O H W
A N Y S N I Y I O W T N Q I O U Y T H N K A T N N I U Y E N M L
W O N T E W Q N V J A L N Q W E R T Y I O P N K H G E N H H A Z
I S W T I Y N I W T R W O R I M M U N E D E F E N S E I I N I E
T G D A B N I N E N B X O N Q W E R T F R D E W B N F D S R W N
I N O I G E T A F L U S H O T N O T E N I W O T O A S V T N I N
K H I Y E N S T T H I M E S Q W E R T Y U I O B M T T T N I N D
A L S Y N I Y R T W Q N M B X B V W T N I S E T D W T I Y O W E
N A I Y I O P T A N D D I X X V B C N I Q T Y G A N J K E O Q N
U E R I X S S V I T A M I N C G T O T E X B Q B N J S B D A C B
N K G N W Z T A B E N I T O K O A M N S G N K H G B D A K W I N
G O N A B C E G H T G F W E A R A M A S K D S A N K O Y A Q E N
T P I C N G I N A M I Y N B E T Q T N I O W O R C O K I N G N I
```

Activity Bank

Directions for the activities utilized in the Let's Practice section are included here. In the lesson plans the instructor will sometimes be referred to the Activity Bank for further explanation.

Brainstorm

1. Students work together to write rules for their class.
2. The instructor will write students' ideas on the board.

Scrambled Sentences

1. Students work with a small group.
2. Students read the paragraph and work together to unscramble the spelling of the underlined words. Students write the word on the line next to the scrambled spelling.
3. Students read their completed paragraph to the class.
4. Instructor may wish to comment on the passage.

Survey

1. Students talk to their classmates. They ask questions about their classmates' weekend, with WHAT, WHERE, and WHO, for example: "Who did you see last weekend?"
2. Students write on their own surveys both their questions and their classmates responses.
3. Go over student results with the class.

How to Conduct a Cloze Listening Activity

1. Read the passage at a normal rate of speed. Remind students this is a real world listening activity so you will not stop during the reading, but you will read as many times as they request. It is not uncommon for students to request 4 or more readings. Students write the missing words on the lines.
2. When finished, ask for volunteers to read sections aloud to check student responses.
3. Where applicable, ask reading comprehension questions about the reading.

Answer Questions about the Conversation

Use the conversation and substitutions. Ask questions. Students write their answers. Go over responses with the class.

Pair, Square, Share

Pairs of students interview each other. After both partners share, each pair then joins another pair to make a group of 4 (a square). The original partners summarize their partner's responses to this group of 4. Continue until all students have summarized their original partner's responses.

Correct/Incorrect Dictation

1. Demonstrate. Have students make two columns on their paper labeled: Correct and Incorrect
2. Dictate the following sentences.
3. Students listen to the sentences and decide if it is correct or incorrect. If the sentence is correct, they should write it under the Correct column.
4. If the sentence is incorrect, they should write it under the Incorrect column.

Note: **Teacher Answer Key in bold.**

How to Prepare a Concentration Game Board and How to Play Concentration

1. Prepare a Concentration board using a piece of poster board and 4x6 index cards folded to make 24 pockets. Attach the pockets to the board. Number each pocket on the pocket face with a marker.
2. Prepare Concentration cards using 3x5 index cards. Write desired responses on individual cards. For example: questions and answers; split sentences; opposites; vocabulary and definitions, etc. Place one card into each of the Concentration board pockets facing away so the writing on the card cannot be seen.
3. Play begins when a student chooses two cards randomly from the pockets and reads the cards aloud to the class. If a student has chosen a match, i.e. a question and its appropriate answer, the cards are removed from the board and the student receives a point. If the two cards chosen do not match, cards are replaced in the board in the same pocket from which they were taken. Next student plays. Play continues until all cards have been properly matched.
4. At conclusion of play, read all matches aloud.

Prepare Concentration cards using split sentences, word and definitions, vocabulary words and their pictures, etc.

Correct/Incorrect Dictation

1. Demonstrate. Have students make two columns on their paper labeled: Correct and Incorrect
2. Dictate the following sentences.

3. Students listen to the sentences and decide if it is correct or incorrect. If the sentence is correct, they should write it under the Correct column.
4. If the sentence is incorrect, they should write it under the Incorrect column.

Note: **Teacher Answer Key in bold.**

<u>How to Play the Add On Game</u>

1. Student 1 makes a statement, for example: "I'm going to the store to buy some apples."
2. Student 2 repeats Student 1's statement and adds his/her own statement, for example, "I'm going to the store to buy some apples and bananas."
3. Continue repeating and adding statements until all have participated.

<u>How to Prepare and Play Beat the Cat</u>

1. This game is similar to the TV show "Wheel of Fortune." Write the letters of the alphabet across the top of the board: A-B-C-D...
2. Draw lines to represent the letters of each word in the puzzle sentence. For example:

_____ _____ _____   _____ _____   _____ _____ _____ _____

3. Students take turns guessing ***consonants*** only.
4. Fill in the guessed consonants that appear in the puzzle. For example:

_____ _____ D   _____ _____   L _____ _____ _____

5. For consonants guessed that do NOT appear in the puzzle, begin drawing a cat, one body part per incorrect consonant, in the following order: head, body, face, whiskers, ears, tail. The addition of the tail indicates the teacher has won! Avoid this by adding paws to the cat if needed!
6. Continue until all consonant spaces are filled in.
7. Students guess which vowels fill the remaining spaces in the puzzle. Fill in their correct vowel guesses. For example: G O D I S L O V E

<u>How to Prepare and Play Mix & Match</u>

1. The instructor creates 3x5 card pairs, for example, vocabulary and definition, sentence halves, opposite words, sentence completions, questions and answers, nouns and the adjectives which modify them, etc.
2. Shuffle cards and distribute one per student.
3. Students mix with each other to find their match.
4. Matched pairs share their matches with the class.

How to Conduct an Interview Line Up

1. Create two equal lines of students facing each other about 2' apart. Designate Line A and B.
2. Instructor gives an interview topic/question for Line A to interview their partner in Line B.
3. When all have completed the interview, the student at the end of Line A moves to the opposite end of Line A while other students in Line A shift one place over. Line B does NOT move. All students now face a new partner.
4. Instructor gives a new interview topic/question. Line B begins the interview.
5. Continue shifting Line A until all students have interviewed each other.

How to Complete the Mystery Word Search

1. First, students complete the sentences using clues from the conversation and substitutions.
2. Second, students write the responses to the exercises in the first part on the lines in the puzzle.
3. Third, students identify the mystery word in the box and write it on the line.

This activity looks a bit like a cross word puzzle. Here's how you can make a puzzle.

Part 1

1. Write fill-in-the-blank sentences using the vocabulary words. Students complete the sentences.

Part 2

2. Create the Mystery Word Search Puzzle. Choose one word to write vertically. Draw a box around this word. Responses to the sentences in Part 1 are written horizontally intersecting the vertical word along a common letter. See example below.
3. Replace the letters of the vertical and horizontal words with blank lines. Write one letter on each line. The vertical word inside the box becomes the mystery word.
4. Students fill in the puzzle with the correct responses from Part 1. The mystery word will appear inside the box.
5. Have students write the mystery word on the line.

Part 1

1. Jesus sat in a **boat**.
2. The man scattered **grain**.
3. Jesus taught a **parable**.
4. The **crowd** was very big.

5. Some **seed** fell on the path.

Part 2

1.					**b**	**o**	**a**	**t**	
2.		g	r	a	**i**	n			
3.			p	a	**r**	a	b	l	e
4.	c	r	o	w	**d**				
5.					**s**	e	e	d	

Write the mystery word in the box here: ***birds***

NOTE: The font used here is Courier New 14 pt. All letters are of equal size so the puzzle lines up perfectly.

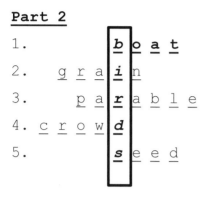

Practicing Perfect Pronunciation

Much of English pronunciation is learned through simple repetition. Even the lowest level beginners can learn to hear and recognize the elements of English pronunciation. Therefore, it's helpful if students are introduced to the elements of English pronunciation from the very beginning of their language acquisition. This text emphasizes Sound Units and Intonation Patterns which are discussed below.

As Repetition Drills are foundational for learning to hear and recognize English pronunciation, a review of how to conduct basic drills follows.

Sound Units

Sound units are chunks of words which flow together and are usually said with one breath. The native English speaking listener will naturally recognize Sound Units of spoken English as the speaker will pause for a brief moment between sound units. We can also use grammar to identify sound units.

English words can be divided into two categories: Content Words and Structure (aka Function) Words.

Content Words	Structure Words
Nouns	Articles
Verbs	Demonstratives
Adjectives	Pronouns
Adverbs	Conjunctions
WH-Question Words	Modals
	To Be Verbs

In spoken English, we accent the Content Words and reduce the Structure Words. Sound Units are built around Content Words and their related Structure Words. Students can learn to hear the Sound Units through repetition drills.

Intonation Patterns

Intonation is the rise and fall of the voice. Native English speakers listen for Intonation Patterns to help reinforce the message of the words. The Intonation Patterns introduced in this text are defined below.

Statement – the voice starts higher and moves downward like going down a staircase through each sound unit in a statement. When the end of the statement is reached, at the period, the voice falls. The Statement Intonation Pattern is used for Statements which do not require a response.

We often use arrows drawn on the text to indicate the direction of voice in the Intonation Pattern. For example, here's a simple Statement:

I Have you lived in Miami all my life.

WH-Question – questions that begin with the WH-Question words: Who, What, Where, When, Why, How, require a response from the listener. The voice begins on a high note, then falls through the middle of the sentence until the last Content word when the voice rises to accent the accented syllable in the last Content word and then falls.

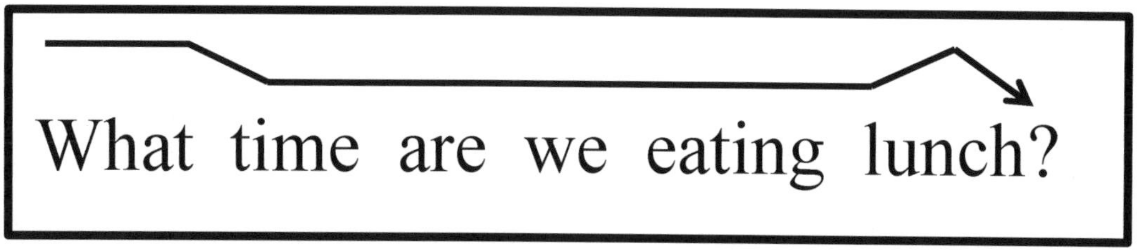

What time are we eating lunch?

YES/NO Question – questions for which Yes or No are the responses. The voice rises at the end of each Sound Unit and raises dramatically at the end of the sentence.

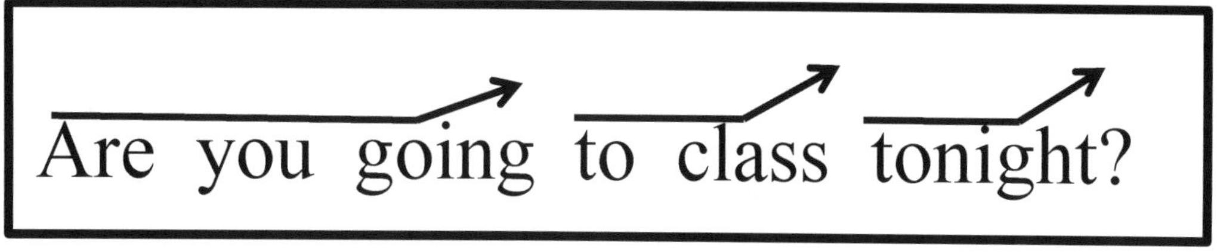

Are you going to class tonight?

Two Items or Choices Connected with AND or OR – Both items are said with equal stress while the word that connects them, AND or OR, is said at a lower pitch. For the first item, raise the voice at the end of the item. For the second item, the voice goes up then down on the end.

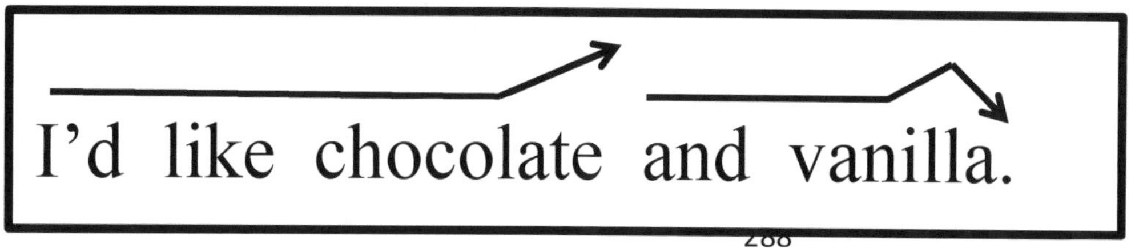

I'd like chocolate and vanilla.

Series of Items – The voice raises at the comma after each item in the list, lowers at AND just before the final item, then drops at the end of the final item as in Statement intonation.

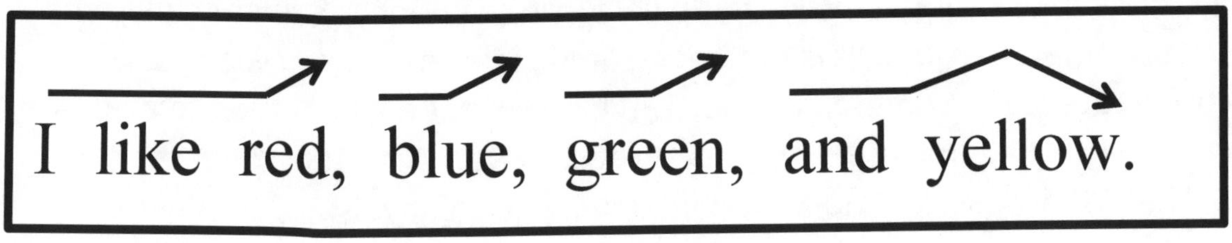

Conducting Drills

How to Conduct a Total Physical Response (TPR) Drill

In TPR, the instructor gives a command, for example, "Close the door." Student closes the door to demonstrate comprehension. It is not necessary for the student to speak; only complete the action requested. Common uses of TPR involve students pointing to a picture or object from among a group of pictures or objects thereby demonstrating their comprehension. The TPR drill is used most often at low language levels.

How to Conduct a Repetition Drill

Repetition Drill is used to teach new vocabulary and to teach vocabulary in sentences. To conduct a repetition drill:

1. Show students a picture or object to introduce the vocabulary.
2. Repeat the word 5-6 times while students listen.
3. Students then repeat the word after the instructor 5-6 times.
4. After drilling 3 words, review.

How to use Backward Build up to Teach a Sentence

Sentences are easier to learn by starting at the end of the sentence and working toward the beginning.

1. The instructor repeats the entire sentence one time, for example: There's a Post Office on Main Street.
2. Then the instructor begins with a repetition drill at the end of the sentence with "Main Street."
3. Next, the preposition 'on' is added and the phrase, "on Main Street" is drilled.
4. Third, the beginning of the sentence is drilled, "There's a Post Office".
5. Finally, the entire sentence is drilled, "There's a Post Office on Main Street."

How to Direct Students to Do the Substitution Drill

The Substitution Drill is useful to 'substitute' additional vocabulary word
that has been drilled already. For example: "There's a **bank** on **New**
conversation then is more useful if Substitute vocabulary is utilized
Substitutions, this text uses **bold underlined words.**

How to Conduct a Question and Answer Chain Drill

In a Chain Drill, all students practice asking and answering questions.

1. To begin, the instructor asks a question to Student 1 who answers the question.
2. Student 1 then asks a question to Student 2 who answers.
3. Continue the chain until all students have both asked and answered a question

ABOUT THE AUTHOR

Professor Barbara Kinney Black began her 25 year ESL teaching career as a volunteer in her church, University Baptist, in Coral Gables, Florida. She had taught for just 3 weeks when it became obvious to her that she could do something she loved for a career. She returned to university for a Master's of Science degree in T.E.S.O.L. Since that time she has taught ESL in a diversity of settings including:

Adult Education – Miami-Dade, Florida

College – Miami-Dade College, Miami, Florida - largest college in the U.S.A.

Seminary – New Orleans Theological Seminary - Miami Campus

China – Honghe University - sharing Western ESL teaching technique with Chinese English Teachers

Professor Black has authored ESL curriculum for a variety of applications including:

ESL for Florida Power and Light employees

ESL for employees of Global Mail Solutions

Co-authored Teaching English Techniques & Practice for Honghe University

Professor Black is the author of the multi-level ESL curriculum for adults

Tried and True ESL Lessons

Tried and True ESL Lessons Time Saving Lesson Plans for Instructors

Tried and True Everyday English from Genesis High Beginner and Intermediate ESL Student

Tried and True Everyday English from Genesis High Beginner and Intermediate ESL Instructor

Professor Black enjoys most her involvement, since 1994, as a teacher/trainer for churches in Florida wishing to begin ESL ministries.

Professor Black has directed two ESL ministries in South Florida churches.

Above all, Professor Black delights in seeing her students succeed.